English Grammar for Students of Japanese

The Study Guide for Those Learning Japanese

Mutsuko Endo Hudson

Michigan State University

The Olivia and Hill Press®

ENGLISH GRAMMAR series
edited by Jacqueline Morton

English Grammar for Students of French
English Grammar for Students of Spanish
English Grammar for Students of German
English Grammar for Students of Italian
English Grammar for Students of Russian
English Grammar for Students of Latin

Gramática Española para Estudiantes de Inglés

ISBN 0-934034-16-8

CONTENTS

TO THE STUDENT

English Grammar for Students of Japanese explains basic terminology and concepts of English grammar, focusing on material which will most benefit students of Japanese.

This handbook is designed to supplement any beginning Japanese language textbook. It is not meant to be comprehensive, nor is it intended to replace a language textbook. It is written to help you get the most out of your Japanese textbook as well as to answer some of the questions you will have as you learn Japanese.

How to Use the English Grammar Handbook

Each short chapter is a self-contained discussion of a particular grammar topic.

- Consult the table of contents and index to find where the grammatical terms and concepts you want explained are covered in this handbook.
- Read the relevant pages carefully, making sure that you understand the explanations and the examples.
- Do the Review, if provided, at the end of the chapter you have read. Compare your answers with the Answer Key at the end of the handbook. If they don't match, review the section.

Tips for Studying a Foreign Language

1. RULES—Make sure you understand each rule before you move on to the next one. Language learning is like building a house; each brick is only as secure as its foundation.

   After you have read the explanation of a new grammatical rule, memorize one good example. It will help you remember the rules in a concrete way. Also, to test your understanding, try to make up simple examples of your own.

2. MEMORIZATION—Memorization plays an important part in language learning. You will have to memorize vocabulary (see Vocabulary below), special phrases, verb conjugations, grammar rules, and so forth. Here are some steps to follow when you memorize new material:

   - Divide the material to be memorized into sections you can easily remember (for instance, two sentences).

- Read the first section aloud several times.
- Write down the first section as you repeat it aloud to yourself.
- Compare what you wrote with the original.
- Repeat the last two steps until there is no difference between what you have written and the original.
- Repeat the steps above to memorize the second section.
- Continue memorizing each section in the same way, reciting from the beginning each time.

Work at memorizing for only short periods of time. If you find you are not concentrating on the material, take a break or do a different part of your assignment.

3. **VOCABULARY**—Use any trick or gimmick that helps you remember. Here are some that students have found useful:

- Write each word on a separate index card: Japanese on one side, the English equivalent on the other. You can draw or paste pictures for some of the objects or actions.
- Use cards or pens of different colors to help you remember useful information. To remember parts of speech, for example, you might use red for nouns, green for verbs, blue for adjectives, and so on.
- There is rarely a perfect one-to-one correspondence between words in English and Japanese. Make a note of important differences in meaning or usage on the cards; ex., **aru** *"to exist* (used with objects only)".
- When learning new words, look at the Japanese side first, then the English equivalent (or picture) on the back. Turn over to the Japanese side again and say the word aloud several times, trying to remember the meaning. It will help if you visualize the objects, actions, events, etc. that you are saying.
- When testing yourself, look at the English (or picture) side of the card and try to remember the Japanese equivalent. Say it aloud and make up short sentences with it. For example, when you see the word *apple*, say **ringo**, **Ringo o tabemasu** *(I eat apples)*, **Ringo ga kirai desu** *(I hate apples)*, or **Ringo wa akai desu** *(The apple is red)*.
- Limit the number of words to be memorized to three or four at a time. When you are confident that you have memorized the first

group, add new words until you have learned all the vocabulary required. As you progress, mix up the cards you have learned and test yourself.

- When you come across words that you don't remember, check the meaning and set them aside in the "troulbe pile". After going through the entire deck, review this group, again setting aside the words giving you trouble. The "trouble pile" will go down each time and eventually there will be none left.

- Shuffle the deck often so that you see the words "cold" (i.e., without remembering their order).

4. **Language tapes**—It is better to listen to tapes for short periods several times during the week rather than doing everything in one long sitting. Before memorizing a dialogue, for example, be sure that you first listen to the correct pronunciation on tape. Listen first to the whole dialogue in order to get the general idea of the content. Then divide the dialogue into sections and memorize them using the tape.

5. **Written exercises**—Read the Japanese words and sentences out loud as you write them. That way you are practicing seeing, saying and hearing the words. It will help you remember them.

6. **Daily practice**—Set aside a block of time each day for studying Japanese. Try not get behind. It's almost impossible to catch up because it takes time to absorb the material and to develop the skills.

7. **Seize the moment**—The goal in learning Japanese is to communicate in the language. Practice speaking with your classmates, teachers and Japanese friends, whenever you can. Keep a journal in Japanese (however simple) and write down what you did and thought that day. Not only will it be fun to express yourself in Japanese, but you will also remember words, phrases and patterns more easily because they will have become truly meaningful.

Ganbatte kudasai ne.

Mutsuko Endo Hudson

INTRODUCTION

When you learn a foreign language, in this case Japanese, you must look at each word in three ways; its **meaning, classification** and **use**.

1. The **meaning** of a word—An English word must be connected with a Japanese word that has an equivalent meaning.

   The English word *apple* has the same meaning as the Japanese word **ringo**.

Words with equivalent meanings are learned by memorizing vocabulary items. Sometimes two words sound very similar in English and Japanese. Japanese has borrowed many words from English; these borrowed or loan words are especially prevalent in food, sports, fashion and technology and are, of course, easy to learn.

English	Japanese
America	Amerika
tennis	tenisu
computer	konpyuuta

Occasionally, knowing one Japanese word will help you learn another.

   Knowing that **yasumi** means *holiday* or *vacation* should help you learn that **yasumimasu** is *to rest,* and knowing that **asobi** means *game* should help you remember that **asobimasu** is *to play.*

Usually there is little similarity between words, and knowing one Japanese word will not help you learn another. As a general rule, you must memorize each vocabulary item separately.

   Knowing that **otoko** is *man* will not help you learn that **onna** is *woman.*

In addition, there are times when words in combination take on a special meaning.

   The Japanese word **hara** means *abdomen* and **tateru** means *to build.* However, **hara o tateru** means *to get angry.*

An expression whose meaning as a whole (**hara o tateru**) is different from the meaning of the individual words (**hara** and **tateru**) is called an **idiom**. You will need to pay special attention to these idiomatic expressions in order to recognize them and use them correctly.

2. The **classification** of a word—English words are classified in nine categories called **parts of speech**. Here is a list of the parts of speech used in English:

noun   article
pronoun   preposition
verb   conjunction
adjective   interjection
adverb

Japanese does not have articles (ex., *a, the*) or prepositions (ex., *at, from*). Somewhat corresponding to prepositions, Japanese has what are called **particles**. Also, it has the **copula**, which is similar to the linking verb *to be* in English. The parts of speech used in Japanese are:

noun   adverb
pronoun   particle
verb   conjunction
copula   interjection
adjective

Each part of speech has its own rules for use. You must learn to recognize the part of speech of a word in order to choose the correct Japanese equivalent and know what rules to apply.

Look at the word *is* in the following sentences:

a. Mr. Suzuki *is* a businessman.
b. Mr. Suzuki *is* in his office now.
c. Mr. Suzuki *is* busy.[1]

The English word *is* is the same in all three sentences, but in Japanese three different words will be used and three different sets of rules will apply because each instance of *is* belongs to a different part of speech.

3. The **use** of a word—A word must also be identified according to the role it plays in the sentence. Each word, whether English or Japanese, plays a specific role. Determining this role or function will also help you to choose the correct Japanese equivalent and to know what rules to apply.

---

[1]a. The copula, see p. 27.
 b. The verb *imasu*, see p. 28.
 c. I-type adjectives, see p. 37.

Look at the word *dog* in the following sentences.

    a. A *dog* is running in the yard.
    b. I got a *dog* for my birthday.
    c. I gave some water to a *dog*.[1]

Because *dog* has a different function in each sentence above, the short word, called a "particle," which is attached to the Japanese equivalent of *dog* will be different in each sentence.

As a student of Japanese you must learn to recognize both the part of speech and the function of each word in a given sentence. The part of speech of a word will determine where you place it in a sentence and the function of a word will determine what particle you must add after it.

Compare the way words are placed in the English sentence below and the way they are placed in the corresponding Japanese sentences.

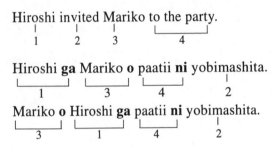

IN ENGLISH
First we say *Hiroshi*, the person who did the inviting, next the word expressing the action *invited*, and then *Mariko*, the person who was invited. If we switch the order of the two participants, the meaning will be quite different: *Mariko invited Hiroshi to the party*.

IN JAPANESE
Identifying the part of speech will tell you which word to place at the end of the sentence. Because it is the verb, **yobimashita** *(invited)* can only be at the end of a sentence.

---

[1]a. Subject, see p. 70.
  b. Direct object, see p. 82.
  c. Indirect object, see p. 82.

Identifying the function of a word in the sentence will tell you whether to use the particle **ga** or **o** after it. The word **Hiroshi**, the person who did the inviting, is followed by **ga**, while the word **Mariko**, the person invited, is followed by **o**. You can say these phrases in either order, as long as they are each followed by the correct particle.

Since parts of speech and function are often determined in the same way in English and in Japanese, this handbook will show you how to identify them in English. You will then learn to compare English and Japanese constructions. This will give you a better understanding of the explanations in your Japanese textbook.

1. WHAT IS A NOUN?

A **noun** is a word that can be the name of a person, an animal, a place, a thing, an event, or an idea.

IN ENGLISH
Let us look at some different types of words which are nouns:

- a person   baby, boy, student, Yoko, Prof. Inoue
- an animal   bear, bird, butterfly, fish, snake, Tweetie
- a place   park, city, White House, Japan, Asia
- a thing   car, shirt, flower, pen, water, Tokyo Tower
- an event or activity   baseball, laundry, party, Kabuki, Christmas
- an idea or concept   happiness, mathematics, truth, Buddhism

As you can see, a noun is not only a word which names something that is tangible, i.e., something that you can touch, such as *car, bird,* and *White House*. It can also be the name of things that are abstract, i.e., something that you cannot touch, such as *happiness, truth*, and *Buddhism*.

A noun that does not state the name of a specific person, place, thing, etc. is called a **common noun**. A common noun does not begin with a capital letter, unless it is the first word of a sentence. All the nouns above that are not capitalized are common nouns.

A noun that is the name of a specific person, place, thing, etc. is called a **proper noun**. A proper noun always begins with a capital letter. All the nouns above that are capitalized are proper nouns.

> Hiroshi is a student.
> | |
> proper noun   common noun

A noun that is made up of two words is called a **compound noun**. A compound noun can be a common noun, such as *comic book, trash can* and *ice cream*, or a proper noun, such as *White House, Tokyo Tower* and the *Narita Airport*.

To help you recognize nouns, look at the paragraph below where the nouns are in *italics*.

> A *shower* swept toward me from the *foot* of the *mountain,* touching the *cedar forests* white, as the *road* began to wind up into

the *pass*. I was nineteen and traveling alone through the *Izu Peninsula*. My *clothes* were of the *sort students* wear, dark *kimono*, high wooden *sandals*, a *school cap*, a *book sack* over my *shoulder*. I had spent three *nights* at hot *springs* near the *center* of the *peninsula*, and now, my fourth *day* out of *Tokyo*, I was climbing toward *Amagi Pass* and *South Izu*

> (Kawabata Yasunari, *The Izu Dancer*, translated by Edward Seidensticker)

A noun can have a variety of functions in a sentence; that is, it can be the subject of the sentence (see **What is a Subject?**, p. 70) or an object (see **What are Objects?**, p. 82).

IN JAPANESE

Nouns are identified the same way as they are in English. In romanized script a proper noun begins with a capital letter. However, the native script does not have a device such as capitalization; you can only determine from the meaning of the word if it is a common noun or a proper noun.

Just as in English, a Japanese noun can have a variety of functions in a sentence.

▼▼▼▼▼▼▼▼▼▼▼▼▼▼▼▼REVIEW▼▼▼▼▼▼▼▼▼▼▼▼▼▼▼▼

Circle the nouns in the following sentences.

1. One spring day Joe and Nancy Smith went to Kyoto by train.
2. The Smiths visited a temple up on a mountain.
3. The temperature was low, but the view was magnificent.
4. The cherry trees were blossoming and the birds were chirping.
5. In the garden some children in school uniform were playing.
6. Their hearts seemed to be filled with joy and happiness.
7. The couple took many pictures.
8. They also bought postcards to send to their friends in America.

2. WHAT IS A PRONOUN?

A **pronoun** is a word used in place of one or more nouns. It may stand, therefore, for a person, an animal, a place, a thing, an event, or an idea (see **What is a Noun?**, p. 5).

Generally a pronoun is used to refer to someone or something that has already been mentioned. In the example below, the pronoun *he* refers to the proper noun *Paul.*

> *Paul* likes to swim. *He* practices every day.

A pronoun is also used to refer to someone or something that the speaker sees at the time of speaking.

> Who is *he*?
> What is *that*?

IN ENGLISH

Pronouns are used extensively. For example, rather than repeating the proper noun "Kathy" in the following two sentences, it is better to use a pronoun in the second sentence.

> *Kathy* went to Japan. *She* particularly enjoyed the old castles.
> instead of saying *Kathy* again

There are different types of pronouns, each serving a different function and following different rules.

PERSONAL PRONOUN—A pronoun that refers to a person or thing (see **What is a Personal Pronoun?**, p. 10).

> *I* like *her*.
> *He* is watching *us*.

REFLEXIVE PRONOUN—A pronoun that reflects the action of the verb back to the subject of the sentence.

> Mary looked at *herself*.
> The players congratulated *themselves*.

INTERROGATIVE PRONOUN—A pronoun that asks a question about a person or a thing (see **What is an Interrogative Word?**, p. 102).

> *Who* wrote this?
> *What* did you buy?

DEMONSTRATIVE PRONOUN—A pronoun that points out a person or a thing (see **What is a Demonstrative Word?**, p. 109).

> *This* is very expensive.
> I prefer *those*.

INDEFINITE PRONOUN—A pronoun that is used to refer to an unidentified person or thing (see **What are Indefinite and Negative Pronouns?**, p. 117).

> *Someone* was here a minute ago.
> I want to drink *something*.

NEGATIVE PRONOUN—A pronoun that is the negative equivalent of an indefinite pronoun; it negates or denies the existence of someone or something (see **What are Indefinite and Negative Pronouns?**, p. 117).

> *Nobody* came today.
> Bill said *nothing* about his future plans.

IN JAPANESE

PERSONAL PRONOUN—Japanese has personal pronouns, but their use is limited and different from English (see **What is a Personal Pronoun?**, p. 10).

> **Watashi** wa terebi o mite imasu.
> *I am watching television.*

> **Kanojo** ni kiite kudasai.
> *Please ask **her.***

REFLEXIVE PRONOUN—Japanese has only one reflexive pronoun **jibun** which is used differently from the reflexive pronouns in English. Consult your textbook for more information.

> **Jibun** o sememashita.
> *I blamed **myself.***

INTERROGATIVE PRONOUN—See **What is an Interrogative Word?**, p. 102.

> **Dare** ga kore o kaita n desu ka.
> ***Who** wrote this?*

> **Nani** o kaimashita ka.
> ***What** did you buy?*

DEMONSTRATIVE PRONOUN—See **What is a Demonstrative Word?**, p. 109.

> **Kore** wa totemo takai desu.
> *This is very expensive.*

> **Are** o kudasai.
> *Please give me **that**.*

INDEFINITE PRONOUN—See **What are Indefinite and Negative Pronouns?**, p. 117.

> Sakki koko ni **dareka** imashita.
> *Someone was here a minute ago.*

> **Nanika** nomitai n desu.
> *I want to drink something.*

[handwritten: watashi wa nehoyo, Want = hanashitai desu]

NEGATIVE PRONOUN—There are no negative pronouns in Japanese. For ways to express meanings similar to those expressed by negative pronouns in English, see **What are Indefinite and Negative Pronouns?**, p. 117.

▼▼▼▼▼▼▼▼▼▼▼▼▼▼▼▼▼REVIEW▼▼▼▼▼▼▼▼▼▼▼▼▼▼▼▼▼

Circle the pronouns in the following sentences.

1. Can you drive me to the airport tonight?

2. Mark is supposed to be back from the trip, but I haven't seen him yet.

3. They heard the news and couldn't believe it.

4. Her kindness and understanding are greatly appreciated by all of us.

3. WHAT IS A PERSONAL PRONOUN?

A **personal pronoun** is a pronoun that refers to a person or thing (see **What is a Pronoun?**, p. 7).

IN ENGLISH
Personal pronouns are divided into the following categories: the person speaking (the **first person**), the person spoken to (the **second person**), and the person or thing spoken about (the **third person**). All personal pronouns (except the second person, *you)* indicate number; that is, they show whether they refer to one person or thing (**singular**) or to more than one person or thing (**plural**). See **What is Meant by Number?**, p. 13.

> *I* like *it* very much.
> | |
> 1st   3rd person
> sing. singular

> Do *you* like the music?
> |
> 2nd person
> singular or plural

> *She* appointed the members.
> |
> 3rd person singular

> *We* must work together.
> |
> 1st person plural

Most personal pronouns also change their form according to the function they have in the sentence: subject, object, or possessive (see **What is a Subject?**, p. 70, **What are Objects?**, p. 82, and **What is the Possessive?**, p. 18).

Here is a list of the personal pronouns in English according to their various functions:

	Subject	Object	Possessive
1st person singular	I	me	my
plural	we	us	our
2nd person singular	you	you	your
plural	you	you	your
3rd person singular	he, she, it	him, her, it	his, her, its
plural	they	them	their

They trust *me*.

3rd person   1st person
plural   singular
subject   object

I want to send *our* pictures to *him*.

1st person   1st person   3rd person
singular   plural   singular
subject   possessive   object

IN JAPANESE

There are many words that correspond to personal pronouns. Their usage, however, is very different from personal pronouns in English. Often when a noun would be replaced by a personal pronoun in English, it is simply omitted in Japanese. For example, in the sentence below it is more common to omit "Mr. Ono" in the second sentence than to replace it with a pronoun. If you suspect that the listener cannot tell from the context who or what is being referred to, you may repeat the noun again instead of using a pronoun.

Ono-san wa oyogu no ga suki desu. Mainichi renshuu shimasu.
Mr. Ono   swim to like   every day practice   do

Mr. Ono likes to swim. He practices every day.

Japanese personal pronouns indicate person and number, but do not change according to function. The function of a pronoun is indicated by the **particle** that follows it: **ga** indicates that the pronoun is a subject and should be translated by the subject form of the English pronoun, the particle **o** indicates that the pronoun is a direct object and should be translated by the object form of the English pronoun, and the particle **no** indicates that the pronoun is a possessive and should be translated by the possessive form of the English pronoun (see **What is a Preposition?**, p. 44).

Here are some examples of the many personal pronouns that exist for each person in Japanese.

	Singular	**Plural**
1st person	watashi *(I)*	watashitachi *(we)*
2nd person	anata *(you)*	anatatachi *(you)*
3rd person	kare *(he)*, kanojo *(she)*	karera *(they)*, kanojotachi *(they)*

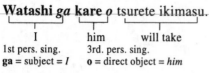

Watashi *ga* **kare** *o* tsurete ikimasu.

I	him	will take
1st pers. sing.	3rd. pers. sing.	
ga = subject = *I*	**o** = direct object = *him*	

*I will take **him**.*

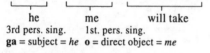

Kare *ga* **watashi** *o* tsurete ikimasu.

he	me	will take
3rd pers. sing.	1st. pers. sing.	
ga = subject = *he*	**o** = direct object = *me*	

*He will take **me**.*

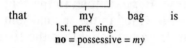

Are wa **watashi** *no* kaban desu.

that	my	bag	is
	1st. pers. sing.		
	no = possessive = *my*		

*That's **my** bag.*

Personal pronouns in Japanese are complicated because the pronoun used will depend on the person spoken to, the person or thing spoken about, and the situation. Consult your textbook.

4. WHAT IS MEANT BY NUMBER?

Number in the grammatical sense means that a word is singular or plural. When a word refers to one person or thing, it is said to be **singular**; when it refers to more than one, it is **plural**.

IN ENGLISH
Many parts of speech indicate number and each follows its own rules to indicate number. Here are just a few examples.

NOUNS (see p. 5)—A singular noun is made plural in a variety of ways:

- by adding "*-s*" or "*-es*"

> one book → two books
> a kiss → many kisses

- by changing its spelling

> man → men
> goose → geese

PRONOUNS (see pp. 7 and 10)—The form of a pronoun depends on whether it refers to one person or thing, or to more than one.

> The book is on the table. *It* is heavy.
> > *It* refers to one object *(book)* → singular pronoun *it*

> The books are on the table. *They* are heavy.
> > *They* refers to more than one object *(books)* → plural pronoun *they*

VERBS (see p. 21)—The form of a verb often changes depending on whether one person is doing the action or more than one.

> Takeshi *studies* in the library.
> > One person is doing the action *(Takeshi)* → singular form of the verb *to study*

> Takeshi and Seiko *study* in the library.
> > More than one person is doing the action *(Takeshi and Seiko)* → plural form of the verb *to study*

DEMONSTRATIVES (see p. 109)—The form of a demonstrative word changes depending on whether you are pointing to one person or thing or to more than one.

> *This* record is expensive.
> > *This* points to one object *(record)* → singular demonstrative *this*

~~*These* records are expensive.~~

These points to more than one object *(records)* → plural demonstrative *these*

IN JAPANESE

In most cases words do not reflect number, regardless of their part of speech. The only time plural number is indicated is when you talk about specific people, but not things or animals. The suffix **tachi** is attached to the noun in such a case.

Kono **hito** wa Furansujin desu.
*This **person** is French.*

Kono hito *(this person)* refers to one specific person → singular noun **hito**

Kono **hitotachi** wa Furansujin desu.
*These **people** are French.*

Kono hitotachi *(these people)* refers to more than one specific person → plural noun **hitotachi**

As you can see, number is only reflected on the word **hito** *(person)*. It is not reflected in **Furansujin** *(French)* because in these sentences the word refers to a nationality, and not to a specific French person or specific French people. Number is never indicated on words like **kono** *(this, these)*.

Uses of a Counter

While in English it is possible to count people, animals, things, abstract concepts, and so on, by simply adding a number such as *one, two, three* (ex. *two students, **ten** pencils, **one** question*), in Japanese a suffix called a **counter** must be attached to the numbers (corresponding more or less to *two people of students*, *ten sticks of pencils*, and *one thing of question)*. (See **What are Prefixes and Suffixes?**, p. 53.)

Let us first look at the way English makes use of counters. It will help you understand the Japanese equivalent.

IN ENGLISH

Since a counter is used to count people, animals, things, and concepts, it is always used with a noun. Depending on what is being counted, English uses a variety of words.

two *groups* of children
  | | |
number counter   noun (people)

a *herd* of sheep
  | |
counter   noun (animals)

a *pack* of lies
  | |
counter noun (abstract concept)

There are many counters used with things:

a *piece* of cake   a *slice* of ham
a *head* of lettuce   a *stalk* of celery
a *cup* of coffee   a *gallon* of milk

Notice that the counter used depends on the noun that follows. For example, we can speak of *a slice of ham*, but not of *a slice of milk*. When we speak about things, the counters used often depend on the appearance of the things. We count thin, flat things with *slices (a slice of bread)* or *sheets (a sheet of paper)* and long things with *stalks (a stalk of celery)* or *sticks (a stick of butter)*. We measure powdery things with *tablespoons* and *cups (a tablespoon of flour)*, and liquids with *cups, bottles, quarts* and *gallons (a cup of water, a gallon of milk)*, and so on.

Counters are often used with numbers. Although the counter changes depending on the noun, the number is always expressed as *one, two, three*, etc,. regardless of the noun that follows.

The order of the words is the following: number + counter + *of* + noun. When the number is *two* and above, the counter adds an "s" but the noun does not change.

They bought *ten sheets of paper.*
                | | |
            number counter noun

I drank *three cups of coffee.*
           | | |
        number counter noun

IN JAPANESE

Unlike English in which counters are independent words usually used with **mass nouns** (nouns that you cannot count, such as liquids and powder), Japanese counters are suffixes which are used with **count nouns** (nouns you can count, such as *pens* and *cars)* as well as mass nouns. Therefore, in the case of count nouns you cannot just say *two pens*, but you must say *two **sticks** of pens* and in the case of mass nouns you cannot just say *three wines*, but you must say *three **bottles** of wine*, and so on.

When expressing a number in Japanese, you will first have to identify the type and shape of the noun which is counted. Here are a few examples of the numbers *one*, *two*, and *three* with various counters:

Noun	Number + counter	
people		
(children, students, women, Americans)	hito-ri	*one*
	futa-ri	*two*
	san-nin	*three*
small animals		
(dogs, cats, fish, flies)	ip-piki	*one*
	ni-hiki	*two*
	san-biki	*three*
thin flat things		
(paper, plates, shirts, toast)	ichi-mai	*one*
	ni-mai	*two*
	san-mai	*three*
long cylindrical things		
(pencils, bottles, cucumbers)	ip-pon	*one*
	ni-hon	*two*
	san-bon	*three*
chunky or global things and concepts		
(boxes, erasers, apples, problems)	hito-tsu	*one*
	futa-tsu	*two*
	mit-tsu	*three*

In a sentence, the regular word order is as follows: noun (N) + particle (P) + number (#) + counter (C). (The particle depends on the function of the noun in the sentence. See **What is a Preposition?**, p. 44.)

Teeburu no ue ni keeki ga **futa-tsu** arimasu.
table   's top on cake   two pieces   are
                        N   P   #   C

Two pieces of cake are on the table.

Teeburu no ue ni pen ga **ni-hon** arimasu.
table   's top on pen   two   are
                      N   P #   C

Two pens *are on the table.*

Your textbook will tell you how to express numbers with many more counters, as well as the rules for their pronunciation. These rules are important since the pronunciation of counters and numbers often changes.

▼▼▼▼▼▼▼▼▼▼▼▼▼▼▼▼REVIEW▼▼▼▼▼▼▼▼▼▼▼▼▼▼▼▼

Next to each noun, write the counters you would use; ex., "**ri, nin**" for people, "**hiki, piki, biki**" for small animals, "**mai**" for flat thin things, "**hon, pon, bon**" for long cylindrical things, and "**tsu**" for chunky or global things and abstract concepts.

1. pen   _____

2. visitor   _____

3. compact disc _____

4. tomato   _____

5. rabbit   _____

6. word   _____

7. baby   _____

8. fish   _____

9. tulip   _____

5. WHAT IS THE POSSESSIVE?

The term **possessive** means that a noun owns or possesses another noun.

IN ENGLISH
You can show possession in one of three ways.

1. An apostrophe can be used after a noun.

  ▪ an apostrophe + "s" is added to a singular possessor

>   *Yoko's* dress
> |
>   singular possessor

>   *Basho's* haiku
>   the *friend's* address
>   a *tree's* branches

  ▪ an apostrophe is added to a plural possessor that ends with an "s"

>   the *students'* teacher
> |
>   plural possessor

>   the *girls'* locker room

2. The word *of* can be used before a noun.

  ▪ *of* is placed before a proper noun possessor

>   the dress *of* Yoko
> |
>   proper noun possessor

>   the haiku *of* Basho

  ▪ *of* is placed before a singular or plural common noun possessor

>   the address *of* a friend
> |
>   singular common noun possessor

>   the branches *of* a tree
>   the teacher *of* the students
> |
>   plural common noun possessor

3. A possessive form of a personal pronoun can be used (see **What is a Personal Pronoun?**, p. 10).

I	→	my	*my* car
		pronoun possessor	
we	→	our	*our* house
you	→	your	*your* camera
he	→	his	*his* teacher
she	→	her	*her* bicycle
it	→	its	*its* goal
they	→	their	*their* children

IN JAPANESE

There is only one way to express possession, and that is by using an equivalent of the possessor + apostrophe + "s" construction (1 above). The Japanese structure is possessor + **no**.

When you want to show possession in Japanese, you must change an English structure using *of* to a structure using an apostrophe + "s".

the dress of Yoko	→	*Yoko's dress*
		possessor
		Yooko-san **no** doresu
the address of a friend	→	*a friend's address*
		tomodachi **no** juusho
the branches of a tree	→	*a tree's branches*
		ki **no** eda

In most cases Japanese nouns do not indicate a singular-plural distinction (see **What is Meant by Number?**, p. 13). In such cases, it makes no difference whether the possessor is singular or plural. The English structure with a plural noun possessor + an apostrophe is translated into a noun + **no**.

singular	*the president of the company*→	*the company's president*
		kaisha **no** shachoo
plural	*the presidents of the companies*→	*companies' presidents*
		kaisha **no** shachoo

The English structure with a possessive pronoun is translated by a pronoun + **no**, which is the same as a noun + **no**.

watashi no kuruma
I   's   car
|
pronoun possessor
1st person singular
my car

kare no sensee
he   's   teacher
|
pronoun possessor
3rd person singular
his teacher

Unlike Japanese nouns, Japanese pronouns make a singular-plural distinction. The plural of the above examples is as follows:

watashitachi no kuruma
we   's   car
|
pronoun possessor
1st person plural
our car

karera no sensee
they   's   teacher
|
pronoun possessor
3rd person plural
their teacher

Note also that, just like pronoun subjects and objects, pronoun possessors are omitted in Japanese when their reference is obvious from the context.

▼▼▼▼▼▼▼▼▼▼▼▼▼▼▼▼REVIEW▼▼▼▼▼▼▼▼▼▼▼▼▼▼▼▼

In the following phrases, underline the word whose Japanese equivalent will be followed by **no**.

1. the parents of Akira

2. the color of a sweater

3. the entrance of the school

4. the speed of a car

5. the covers of the magazines

6. WHAT IS A VERB?

A **verb** is a word that indicates "the action" of the sentence. The word "action" is used in its broad sense, not necessarily physical action.

> Emiko *runs* every day.
> Problems *abound.*

Here are some terms used to talk about verbs:

DICTIONARY FORM—The form under which a verb appears in a dictionary is called the dictionary form (see **What is Meant by Inflection?**, p. 59).

INFLECTION—The various forms which a verb can take are called the inflection of a verb (see **What is Meant by the Inflection of a Verb?**, p. 61).

TENSE—A verb indicates tense, that is, the time (present, past or future) of the action (see **What is Meant by Tense?**, p. 132).

VOICE—A verb shows voice, that is, the relation between the subject and the action of the verb (see **What is Meant by Active and Passive Voice?**, p. 153).

IN ENGLISH
Let us look at different types of words which are verbs:

- a physical activity   to run, to hit, to talk, to walk, to play
- a mental activity   to hope, to believe, to imagine, to think
- a state of being   to be, to lack, to have, to resemble, to seem

To help you learn to recognize verbs, look at the excerpt from a novel below where the verbs are in *italics.* As you can see, the verb can be in the middle or at the end of a sentence.

> I *needed* to *know,* so I *asked* him with my eyes. Do you still *have* a place in your heart for me?

> He *smiled* and *said,* "You *take* care of yourself." I could *see* a look of concern in his eyes, but that *was* it.

> "Yes, sir, I'll *try,*" I *answered.* I *waved* good-bye and *turned* to *go.* The feeling *fades* away and *vanishes* in some distant, boundless place.

> (Yoshimoto Banana, *Kitchen*, translated by Ann Sherif)

The verb is one of the most important words in a sentence; you cannot express a complete thought without a verb (see **What are Sentences** and Clauses?, p. 89). It is important that you learn to identify verbs because the function of words in a sentence often depends on their relationship to the verb. For instance, the subject of a sentence is often the word doing the action of the verb and the object is the word receiving the action of the verb (see **What is a Subject?**, p. 70, and **What are Objects?**, p. 82).

SUBJECT OFTEN does ACTION OF the verb. OBJECT - RECIEVES the ACTION

Teruo hit the ball.

> Teruo → **subject** → doer of the action
> hit → **verb** → action
> ball → **object** → receiver of the action

There are two types of verbs, transitive and intransitive, depending on whether or not they take a direct object.

A **transitive verb** is a verb which takes a direct object. It is indicated by the abbreviation *v.t.* (verb transitive) in dictionaries.

> The pitcher *threw* the ball.
>   v.t.   direct object

> She *quit* her job.
>   v.t.   direct object

An **intransitive verb** is a verb that does not take a direct object. It is indicated by the abbreviation *v.i.* (verb intransitive) in dictionaries.

> He *is sleeping*.
>   v.i.

> Ms. Ito *will arrive* soon.
>   v.i.   adverb

Many verbs can be used transitively or intransitively in sentences, depending on whether they have a direct object or not.

> The students *speak* Japanese.
>   v.t.   direct object

> Actions *speak* louder than words.
>   v.i.   adverb

IN JAPANESE
For the most part the meaning expressed by Japanese verbs is similar to the one expressed by English verbs. However, unlike English where the verb does not have a set place, in Japanese the verb is always placed at the end of the sentence.

All Japanese verbs end in the sound **u** in the dictionary form. Japanese verbs change according to various factors discussed under **What is Meant by the Inflection of a Verb?**, p. 61. Memorizing all the forms for every verb would be an endless task. Fortunately, all but two are regular as opposed to irregular verbs.

Irregular verbs are verbs whose forms do not follow any regular pattern and must be memorized individually. The two irregular verbs are **kuru** *(to come)* and **suru** *(to do)*.

Regular verbs are verbs whose forms follow a regular pattern. Only one example must be memorized and the pattern can then be applied to other verbs in the same group. There are two major groups among the regular verbs:

- **ru** verbs (also called **vowel stem verbs**) are verbs which end in the sound **iru** or **eru** in the dictionary form. (Consult your textbook for exceptions.)

- **u** verbs (also called **consonant stem verbs**) are verbs which are neither the irregular nor **ru** verbs.

As in English, Japanese has transitive and intransitive verbs, but the same verb form cannot be used transitively and intransively. Many Japanese verbs have two different forms; one form to be used when the verb has a direct object and another form when the verb does not.

transitive		intransitive	
akeru	*open something*	aku	*something opens*
hajimeru	*begin something*	hajimaru	*something begins*
ugokasu	*move something*	ugoku	*something moves*

Masako *opens* the door.
    v.t.   direct object
    akeru

The store *opens* early.
    v.i.
    aku

The teacher *begins* the class.
    v.t.   direct object
    hajimeru

The class *begins* at nine o'clock.
    v.i.
    hajimaru

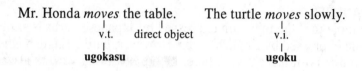

Careful

In English it is possible to change the meaning of a verb by placing short words such as prepositions or adverbs after them (see **What is a Preposition?**, p. 44, and **What is an Adverb?**, p. 40). For instance, the verb *look* in Column A below changes meaning depending on the word that follows it:

Column A		Column B
to look *for*	=	to search for I *am looking for* my key.
to look *after*	=	to take care of I *am looking after* the children.
to look *out*	=	to beware of *Look out* for cars.
to look *into*	=	to investigate I *am looking into* his disappearance.

In Japanese, it is impossible to change the meaning of a verb by adding short words as in Column A. In each sentence above, you would have to use an entirely different verb. When looking up verbs in the dictionary, be sure to look for the specific meaning of the verb. For instance, all the examples above under Column A will be found under the dictionary entry *look*, but you will have to search for the expressions *look for*, *look after*, etc. to find the correct Japanese equivalent. Don't select the first entry under *look* and then add on the Japanese equivalent for *for, after*, etc.; the result will be meaningless in Japanese.

> *I am looking for my key.*
> Kagi **o sagashite imasu.**

> *I am looking after the children.*
> Kodomo **no sewa o shite imasu.**

▼▼▼▼▼▼▼▼▼▼▼▼▼▼▼▼▼REVIEW▼▼▼▼▼▼▼▼▼▼▼▼▼▼▼▼▼

Circle the verbs in the following sentences.

1. This car runs extremely well.

2. Mr. and Mrs. Suzuki were happy.

3. They enjoyed the movie, but they preferred the book.

4. Shinji ate dinner, finished his novel, and then went to bed.

5. Emiko suddenly realized that she has an exam tomorrow.

6. The Prime Minister felt sick yesterday, but today he seems fine.

7. The anxious parents stayed home because they expected a phone call.

8. It was sad to see the little dog struggle to get out of the lake.

9. The price of food increases, but my salary remains the same.

7. WHAT ARE THE USES OF THE VERB "TO BE"?

The verb *to be* has many uses as a main verb or as an auxiliary verb.

"To be" as a Main Verb

IN ENGLISH
To be has the forms *am, are* and *is* in the present tense, and *was* and *were* in the past tense (see **What is Meant by Tense?**, p. 132). In conversation we often shorten *I'm* for *I am*, *it's* for *it is*, *they're* for *they are*, and so on. These are called the **contracted forms** of the verb.

> *I'm* twenty years old.
> *There's* a book on the shelf.

When the verb *to be* links the subject with a noun, an adjective or a prepositional phrase, it is called a **linking verb** or a **copula** (see **What is a Subject?**, p. 70). As a linking verb, *to be* is used in a variety of ways.

- to identify objects and people

> This *is* a word processor.
> I *am* Paul Johnson.

- to identify professions

> Mr. and Mrs. Yamada *were* lawyers.

- to tell ages and time

> I *am* twenty years old.
> It *is* four o'clock.

- to describe the traits and characteristics of a person, place, or thing

> The children *are* healthy.
> The dormitory *was* quiet.

- to give locations

> The books *are* on the shelf.
> The family *was* in Tokyo.

IN JAPANESE

Unlike *be* in English which is a verb, the Japanese equivalent, usually referred to as the **copula**, is not a verb, but a part of speech in its own right. It is one of the three types of words which can function as a **main predicate** in Japanese, the other two being verbs and **i**-type adjectives (see **What is a Predicate?**, p.79). Like the other main predicates, the copula is placed at the end of a sentence, and has polite and plain forms, nonpast and past tense forms, and affirmative and negative forms. (See **What is Meant by Polite and Plain Forms?**, p. 57, **What is Meant by Tense?**, p. 132, and **What are Affirmative and Negative Sentences?**, p. 92).

Here are examples of the polite nonpast and past affirmative forms of the copula (for examples of negative forms, see **What is Meant by the Inflection of the Verb "To be?,"** p. 65).

> Chichi wa gishi **desu**.
> polite nonpast affirmative
> *My father is an engineer.*

> Chichi wa gishi **deshita**.
> polite past affirmative
> *My father was an engineer.*

The copula is used with nouns and **na**-type adjective stems (see p. 37) and, just like the English verb *be*, expresses various meanings.

- to identify objects and people

> Kore wa waapuro **desu**.
> *This is a word processor.*

> Watashi wa Pooru Jonson **desu**.
> *I am Paul Johnson.*

- to identify professions

> Yamada-san wa bengoshi **desu**.
> *Ms. Yamada is a lawyer.*

- to tell ages and time

> Watashi wa hatachi **desu**.
> *I am twenty years old.*

> Ima yo-ji **desu**.
> *It is four o'clock now.*

- to describe the traits and characteristics of a person, place, or thing

    Kodomotachi wa genki **desu**.
    |
    na-type adjective
    The children are healthy.

- to give locations

    Hon wa tsukue no ue **desu**.
    |_____|
    location
    The book is on the desk.

Careful

1. The English expressions *there is* and *there are* do not use a coplua in equivalent Japanese sentences. They can only be expressed with the verb **arimasu** (when referring to things) or **imasu** (when referring to people or animals).

    Tsukue no ue ni hon ga **arimasu**.
    |
    thing
    ***There is** a book on the desk.*
    |
    thing

    Kyooshitsu ni gakusee ga **imasu**.
    |
    people
    ***There are** students in the classroom.*
    |
    people

2. In addition to the polite form copula **desu** used with nouns and **na**-type adjective stems, as seen above, there is another **desu** which is used in the polite form of **i**-type adjectives. Do not confuse the two types of **desu** because they are different. In the plain style, for example, the copula **desu** is replaced by **da**, while **desu** used with **i**-type adjectives is deleted. (**Da** can never be used with **i**-type adjectives.)

	The dormitory is quiet.
polite form	Ryoo wa shizuka **desu**.
	na-type polite form of
	adjective the copula
plain form	Ryoo wa shizuka **da**.
	na-type plain form of
	adjective the copula

The dormitory is big.

polite form   Ryoo wa ookii **desu**.

polite form of the
i-type adjective

plain form   Ryoo wa ookii. (There is nothing after **ookii**, *big*).

plain form of the
i-type adjective

3. Some English expressions with the verb *be* + adjective are translated into Japanese with a main verb + the auxiliary verb **imasu**, and not with the copula **desu**.

I am hungry.   Onaka ga suite **imasu**.

to be adjective   main verb   auxiliary verb

Mr. Ono is tired.   Ono-san wa tsukarete **imasu**.

to be adjective   main verb   auxiliary verb

Your textbook will identify special expressions like these. Be sure to memorize them.

"To be" as an Auxiliary Verb

An **auxiliary verb**, also called a **helping verb**, is a verb which supplements another verb called **the main verb** (see **What is an Auxiliary Verb?**, p. 31).

IN ENGLISH

The verb *be* is used as an auxiliary to form the progressive tenses and the passive voice.

The **progressive tenses** consist of the verb *be* appearing in various tenses + the *-ing* form of the main verb (see **What is the Progressive?**, p. 146).

I *am reading*.   *am* → auxiliary verb in present tense

to be main verb

The **passive voice** consists of the verb *be* in various tenses + the past participle of the main verb (see What is **Meant by Active and Passive Voice?**, p. 153).

Everyone *was invited*.   *was* → auxiliary verb in past tense

to be main verb

IN JAPANESE

The copula **desu** is not used as an auxiliary.

The Japanese equivalent of the progressive construction is the **te** form of the main verb (literally, *do... and*) + the auxiliary verb **imasu** (literally, *exist*).

> *I am reading a book.*
> Hon o yonde **imasu**.
> book   reading   am
> | |
>   main verb   auxiliary verb

For the passive, Japanese uses a special form called the **passive form** of a main verb (see **What is Meant by Active and Passive Voice?**, p. 153).

> *Everyone was invited.*
> Minna **yobaremashita**.
> everyone   was invited
> |
>   main verb in the passive form

▼▼▼▼▼▼▼▼▼▼▼▼▼▼▼▼▼REVIEW▼▼▼▼▼▼▼▼▼▼▼▼▼▼▼▼▼

I. Circle the forms of the verb *to be* in the following sentences.

1. My name is Chris and I'm a friend of Kim's.

2. The people I met at the party were all friendly.

3. Mr. Yoshida was an accountant before he retired.

4. The suspect they're looking for is a tall, skinny person.

5. Our apartment is small, but it's quite comfortable.

II. In the following sentences, can the words in italics be translated with a form of **desu** in Japanese? Circle "Yes" or "No".

1. I *am* the president of the student club.   YES   NO

2. There *are* a lot of national parks around here.   YES   NO

3. This haiku *was* written by Basho.   YES   NO

4. The document *is* in the cabinet.   YES   NO

5. Everyone *is* looking for a summer job now.   YES   NO

8. WHAT IS AN AUXILIARY VERB?

A verb is called an **auxiliary verb** or **helping verb** when it helps or supplements another verb called the **main verb**. While the main verb expresses an action or a state central to the sentence, an auxiliary verb gives a perspective on the main verb.

Many auxiliary verbs function as a main verb when they are used alone.

Mary *is* a teacher.	*is*	→	**main verb**
Paul *has* a headache.	*has*	→	**main verb**
They ***have** gone* to the movies.	***have***	→	**auxiliary verb**
	gone	→	**main verb**
He ***has been*** gone two weeks.	***has***	→	**auxiliary verb**
	been	→	**auxiliary verb**
	gone	→	**main verb**

IN ENGLISH
There are many auxiliary verbs. They have four primary uses:

1. to indicate the tense of the main verb, such as present progressive, past progressive, future, and present perfect tenses (see **What is Meant by Tense?**, p. 132, **What is the Progressive?**, p. 146); ex. *be, will, have*

present progressive	Mary *is reading.* aux. verb main verb
past progressive	Mary *was reading.* aux. verb main verb
future	Mary *will read* a book. aux. verb main verb
present perfect	Mary *has read* the book. aux. verb main verb

2. to help form the passive voice (see **What is Meant by Active and Passive Voice?**, p. 153); ex. *is, are, was*

active	A famous architect *designed* the house.
passive	The house *was designed* by a famous architect. aux. verb main verb

3. to help formulate questions; (see **What are Declarative and Interrogative Sentences?**, p. 97); ex. *do, does, did*

statement   Bob *likes* dogs.

question   ***Does*** Bob *like* dogs?
                 | |
             aux. verb main verb

statement   They *talked* on the phone.

question   ***Did*** they *talk* on the phone?
                | |
             aux. verb main verb

4. to express the speaker's perspective and attitude; ex. *can, may, must, should*

It ***may rain*** tomorrow.
    | |
aux. verb main verb

I ***can*** *speak* German.
  | |
aux. verb main verb

IN JAPANESE

As in English, many verbs can function as both main and auxiliary verbs. However, the function of Japanese auxiliaries is different from that of English auxiliaries: they simply add a supplementary meaning to the main verb. The Japanese auxiliaries indicate the style (plain or polite), the tense (nonpast or past), and the affirmative-negative distinction of the sentence. They are placed at the end of a sentence, following the main verb that always appears in the **te** form. The **te** form of a verb literally means *do... and*, and does not indicate tense.

Let us look at examples of verbs that can be used as auxiliary verbs, as well as main verbs. Notice that these verbs change meaning when they change function. All the sentences below are in the polite style, nonpast tense, and affirmative.

main verb   **imasu**   *there is + person, animal*
auxiliary verb   main verb-**te imasu**   *is doing...*

Kodomo ga **imasu**.
          |
        main verb
There is *a child.*

Yuki ga *futte* **imasu**.
       main verb auxiliary verb
       furu *(fall)*

Snow is falling.
It is snowing.

main verb	**arimasu**	*there is + thing*
auxiliary verb	main verb-**te arimasu**	*is in a state of...*

Ginkoo ga **arimasu**.
         main verb

***There is** a bank.*

Doa ga *akete* **arimasu**.
     main verb auxiliary verb
     akeru *(open)*

*The door **is open**.*

main verb	**mimasu**	*to see*
auxiliary verb	main verb-**te mimasu**	*to try doing...*

Eega o **mimasu**.
     main verb

*I **see** movies.*

Seetaa o *kite* **mimasu**.
    main verb auxiliary verb
    kiru *(wear)*

*I'll **try wearing** the sweater.*

main verb	**agemasu**	*to give*
auxiliary verb	main verb-**te agemasu**	*to do a favor of doing...*

Kodomo ni hon o **agemasu**.
          main verb

*I'll **give** a book to the child.*

Kodomo ni hon o *yonde* **agemasu**.
        main verb auxiliary verb
        yomu *(read)*

*I'll **do the favor of reading** a book for the child.*

English auxiliary verbs such as *do, does, did*, or *will* do not exist as auxiliary verbs in Japanese. Their meaning is conveyed either by a different structure (see **What are Declarative and Interrogative Sentences?**, p. 97) or by suffixes (see **What are Prefixes and Suffixes?**, p. 53, and the chapters dealing with various tenses).

▼▼▼▼▼▼▼▼▼▼▼▼▼▼▼▼REVIEW▼▼▼▼▼▼▼▼▼▼▼▼▼▼▼▼

Cross out the English auxiliary verbs which are not used as auxiliaries in Japanese.

1. Did the children do their homework?

2. They will do their homework tomorrow.

3. Do you want to do your homework now?

4. Have the children done their homework?

9. WHAT IS AN ADJECTIVE?

An **adjective** is a word that describes a noun or a pronoun.

IN ENGLISH

Adjectives are classified according to the way they describe a noun or pronoun.

DESCRIPTIVE ADJECTIVE—An adjective which indicates a quality (see **What is a Descriptive Adjective?**, p. 36).

> Yukiko read an *interesting* novel.
> The flowers are *pretty*.

INTERROGATIVE ADJECTIVE—An adjective which asks a question about someone or something (see **What is an Interrogative Word?**, p. 102).

> *What* book is lost?
> *Which* people did you speak to?

DEMONSTRATIVE ADJECTIVE—An adjective which points out someone or something (see **What is a Demonstrative Word?**, p. 109).

> *This* paper is excellent.
> *That* student is very hardworking.

IN JAPANESE

Adjectives are classified the same way as in English. For more on Japanese adjectives see the chapters listed above and **What is Meant by the Inflection of an Adjective?**, p. 68.

▼▼▼▼▼▼▼▼▼▼▼▼▼▼▼▼▼REVIEW▼▼▼▼▼▼▼▼▼▼▼▼▼▼▼▼▼

Fill in the blanks.

An adjective is a word that describes a (1) _____ or a

pronoun, not a verb. An adjective that describes is called a

(2) _____ adjective. An adjective that asks a question

about someone or something is called an (3) _____

adjective, and an adjective that points out someone or something is

called a (4) _____ adjective.

10. WHAT IS A DESCRIPTIVE ADJECTIVE?

A **descriptive adjective** is a word that indicates a quality of a noun or a pronoun. As the name implies, it *describes* the noun or pronoun.

IN ENGLISH
Descriptive adjectives are divided into two groups depending on how they are connected to the noun or pronoun which they describe: attributive adjectives and predicate adjectives.

ATTRIBUTIVE ADJECTIVE—An **attributive adjective** is connected directly to the noun it describes and always precedes it. We say that an attributive adjective "modifies" the noun or pronoun that follows it.

> The *good* workers were rewarded.
>   adjective   noun described

> The family bought a *new* car.
>   adjective noun described

PREDICATE ADJECTIVE—A **predicate adjective** is connected to the noun or pronoun (i.e., the subject of the sentence) that it describes by a linking verb, usually a form of *to be*. A predicate adjective always comes after the noun or pronoun.

> The workers are *good*.
>   noun   linking
>   subject verb predicate adjective

> The car is *new*.
>   noun   linking
> subject verb predicate adjective

Nouns Used as Adjectives

A noun is sometimes used to modify another noun. In such a case, we say that the first noun is being used as an adjective.

Japanese is interesting.	The *Japanese* class is crowded.
noun	adjective noun
I use a computer.	I use a *computer* software.
noun	adjective noun

IN JAPANESE
Based on their form, Japanese descriptive adjectives are classified into two types: the **i-type adjectives** and the **na-type adjectives**. According to their function in a sentence, both types can be used as attributive or predicate adjectives.

ATTRIBUTIVE ADJECTIVE—As in English, an attributive adjective is placed before the noun it describes. Here is an example of the attributive forms of an **i**-type and a **na**-type adjective.

- **i**-type adjectives (end with the sound "i")

> **Atarashii** kuruma ga arimasu.
> new   car   there is
> | |
> **i**-type adj. noun described
>
> *There is a **new** car.*

- **na**-type adjectives (end with the sound "na")

> **Rippa na** kuruma ga arimasu.
> stately   car   there is
> | |
> **na**-type adj. noun described
>
> *There is a **stately** car.*

PREDICATE ADJECTIVE—As in English, a predicate adjective is placed after the noun or pronoun (i.e., the subject) it describes.

- **i**-type adjectives—They are like verbs in the sense that they change their form according to style, tense, and the affirmative-negative distinction (see **What is Meant by the Inflection of an Adjective?**, p. 68). Here are examples in the plain and polite style, nonpast, affirmative.

Plain nonpast affirmative form—nothing is added to the adjective.

> Kuruma wa **atarashii**.
> | |
> noun   **i**-type adjective
> subject predicate adjective
>
> *The car is **new**.*

Polite nonpast affirmative form—the polite marker **desu** (not to be confused with the copula **desu**, see p. 28) is added after the adjective.

> Kuruma wa **atarashii desu**.
> | | |
> noun   **i**-type adj.   polite marker
> subject predicate adj.
>
> *The car is **new**.*

- **na**-type adjectives (also called **adjectival nouns**)—They are like adjectives in English; they do not change their form. Instead, it is the copula that is attached to them that changes (see p. 65). Here are examples in the plain and polite style, nonpast, affirmative.

Plain nonpast affirmative form—**na** is replaced by the plain form of the copula **da**.

> Kuruma wa **rippa da**.
> | | |
> noun   **na**-type adj. copula
> subject predicate adj.
>
> *The car is **stately**.*

Polite nonpast affirmative form—**na** is replaced by the polite form of the copula **desu** (not to be confused with the polite marker **desu** used with **i**-type adjectives).

> Kuruma wa **rippa desu**.
> | | |
> noun   **na**-type adj. copula
> subject predicate adj.
>
> *The car is **stately**.*

Careful

In Japanese, when a noun is used to describe another noun, it remains a noun and does not become an adjective as it does in English. In such a case, the particle **no** is attached to the first noun.

Nihongo wa omoshiroi desu. noun	**Nihongo no** kurasu noun noun
Japanese is interesting.	*Japanese class*
Konpyuuta o tsukaimasu. noun	**konpyuuta no** sofutowea noun noun
I use a computer.	*computer software*

Summary

Here is a chart that you can use as reference for Japanese descriptive adjectives.

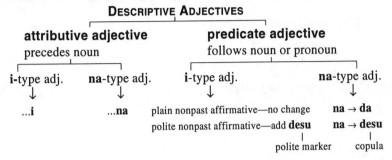

▼▼▼▼▼▼▼▼▼▼▼▼▼▼▼▼▼▼REVIEW▼▼▼▼▼▼▼▼▼▼▼▼▼▼▼▼▼▼

Circle the adjectives in the following sentences.
- Draw an arrow from the adjective you circled to the noun or pronoun described.

1. The game was very exciting.

2. The young woman was reading a newspaper on the crowded train.

3. We were very tired after our long walk.

4. Bill looked great in his dark suit yesterday.

5. The earth is getting warmer year by year.

11. WHAT IS AN ADVERB?

An **adverb** is a word that describes a verb, an adjective, or another adverb. Adverbs indicate manner, time, place, quantity or degree.

Mary drives *well*.
   | |
  verb   adverb
described

The house is *very* large.
          | |
        adverb adjective
               described

I ate *too quickly*.
      | |
    adverb adverb
         described

IN ENGLISH

An adverb can precede or follow the word that it modifies. Here are some examples of different types of adverbs.

- adverbs of manner—These adverbs answer the question *how?* They are the most common adverbs and can usually be recognized by their **-ly** ending.

   Laura sings *beautifully*.
        |
   verb described

   The economy recovered *rapidly*.

- adverbs of time—These adverbs answer the question *when?*

   He will come *soon*.
        |
   verb described

   The guests arrived *late*.

- adverbs of place—These adverbs answer the question *where?*

   The chairperson looked *around*.
                 |
   verb described

   Some people were left *behind*.

- adverbs of quantity or degree—These adverbs answer the question *how much?* or *to what extent?*

Joe sleeps *little* these days.
    verb described

My children do *very* well in school.

Sometimes in English the same word can be used both as an adverb and an adjective.

It is a *fast* train.
    Fast modifies the noun *train*; it is an adjective.

They run *fast*.
    Fast modifies the verb *run*; it describes how they run; it is an adverb.

It is important that you distinguish an adverb from an adjective because they will be different words in Japanese.

IN JAPANESE

As in English, an adverb modifies a verb, an adjective or another adverb, and indicates manner, time, place, quantity or degree. Unlike English, however, the adverb always precedes the word that it describes.

Totemo takai desu.
    adverb adjective described

*It's **very** expensive.*
    adverb adjective described

Yukkuri hanashite kudasai.
    adverb verb described

*Please speak **slowly**.*
    verb adverb
          described

There are three main types of adverbs in Japanese classified according to the part of speech from which they are derived: pure adverbs not derived from other words, adverbs derived from adjectives and nouns, and nouns used as adverbs.

PURE ADVERBS—These words are not derived from other words and are always used as adverbs.

Michiko-san wa **hakkiri** kotaemashita.
                adverb verb described

*Michiko answered **clearly**.*

Kono hen wa **motto** benri desu.
             adverb adjective described

*This area is **more** convenient.*

ADVERBS DERIVED FROM ADJECTIVES AND NOUNS—Japanese adjectives can be changed into adverbs by changing the last sound. This roughly corresponds to forming an adverb by adding *-ly* to an adjective in English.

- i-type adjective → adverb: replace the last sound "i" with "ku"; ex. **tsuyoi** *(strong)* → **tsuyoku** *(strongly)*

> Keekan wa doa o **tsuyoku** oshimashita.
>   adverb   verb described
> *The policeman pushed the door hard (= strongly).*

Note: The **i**-type adjective "**ii**" *(good)* is an exception; its adverb form is **yoku** *(well)*.

> **Yoku** wakarimashita.   Kore wa **ii** hon desu.
> adverb   verb described   adj. noun described
> *I understood well.*   *This is a good book.*

- **na**-type adjective → adverb: replace the last sound "**na**" with "**ni**"; ex. **shizuka na** *(quiet)* → **shizuka** *ni (quietly)*

> **Shizuka ni** arukinasai.
>   adverb   verb described
> *Walk quietly.*

- noun → adverb: add the particle **ni** after the noun, the whole phrase (i.e., the noun + particle) functions as an adverb; ex. **hajime** *(beginning)* → **hajime** *ni (firstly, at first)*.

> **Hajime ni** oshiro o mimashita.
> noun   particle   verb described
>   └── adverb
> *We saw the castle first.*

NOUNS USED AS ADVERBS—Some nouns expressing time or quantity can be used as adverbs, without adding particles.

> Nishida-san wa **ashita** kimasu.
>   noun used verb
>   as adverb
> *Ms. Nishida will come tomorrow.*

> Koora ga **sukoshi** arimasu.
>   noun used   verb
>   as adverb
> *There is some cola.*

Careful

1. The same word cannot function as both an adjective and an adverb in Japanese. For example, to express the English word *fast*, which can function as both an adjective and adverb, **hayai** is used for the adjective and **hayaku** for the adverb.

Hayai densha desu.   Densha wa **hayai** desu.
adjective noun   noun   adjective
It is a fast train.   *The train is fast.*

Hayaku hashiremasu.
adverb   verb
I can run fast.

2. Even though English uses an adjective after the verb *become,* in Japanese the adverb form of a noun or adjective must be used with the verb **narimasu** *(to become).*

Kodomo wa **ookiku** narimashita.
adverb   verb
The child has become big.
verb   adjective

Imooto wa **kookoosee ni** narimasu.
noun   particle   verb
adverb
My sister will become a high school student.
verb   noun

▼▼▼▼▼▼▼▼▼▼▼▼▼▼▼▼▼REVIEW▼▼▼▼▼▼▼▼▼▼▼▼▼▼▼▼▼

Circle the adverbs in the following sentences.
- Draw an arrow from the adverb to the word it describes.

1. The guests arrived quite early.

2. The mechanic fixed my car really quickly.

3. The trip was too long.

4. He has a reasonably secure income.

5. Jennifer is a good student who speaks Japanese very well.

12. WHAT IS A PREPOSITION?

A **preposition** is a word that shows the relationship of one word (usually a noun or pronoun) to another word in the sentence. Prepositions indicate various meanings such as location, time, and means.

IN ENGLISH

The noun or pronoun which is introduced by a preposition is called the **object of the preposition**. Here are examples of prepositions expressing various meanings.

- location

> Bob was *in* the office.
> I bought a coat *at* the department store.
> My roommate put her keys *on* the table.

- direction

> Naomi went *to* school.
> The students came directly *from* class.

- time

> It snows a lot *in* winter.
> *Before* the game, they sang the national anthem.

- indirect object (see **What are Objects?**, p. 82)

> Kazuko gave a necklace *to* her friend.

- means

> Most people commute to work *by* subway.
> Tom sliced the bread *with* a knife.
> I wrote my name *in* katakana.

- partner

> Mr. Yasuda went for a jog *with* his wife.
> Compare this *to* that.

- purpose

> Mr. Yasuda went *for* a jog with his wife.
> I bought books *for* my class.

- possession

> the picture *of* my family
> a work *of* a genius

Some prepositions consist of more than one word:

because of   in front of   instead of
due to   in spite of   on account of

In all the sentences above, the preposition comes before its object. However, the position of a preposition in an English sentence may vary. Spoken English often places a preposition at the end of the sentence; in this position it is called a **dangling preposition**. In formal English there is a strong tendency to avoid dangling prepostions by placing them with the associated noun or pronoun.

Spoken English	→	**Formal English**
The man I spoke *to* is Japanese.		The man *to whom* I spoke is Japanese.
Who are you going out *with*?		*With whom* are you going out?
Here is the book you asked *about*.		Here is the book *about which* you asked.

IN JAPANESE

Roughly corresponding to prepositions in English, Japanese has **postpositions** (so called because they are positioned after a noun or pronoun), which are usually called **particles** in textbooks.[1] You will have to memorize particles as vocabulary items.

Like English prepositions, Japanese particles can express various meanings.

- location

Bobu-san wa kaisha **ni** imashita.
Bob   office in was
*Bob was **in** the office.*

- direction

Naomi-san wa gakkoo **e** ikimashita.
Naomi   school to went
*Naomi went **to** school.*

- time

Fuyu **ni** takusan yuki ga furimasu.
winter in a lot   snow   falls
*It snows a lot **in** winter.*

---

[1]Unlike English prepositions, some Japanese particles are attached to clauses and sentences (see **What are Sentences and Clauses?**, p. 89).

- indirect object (see **What are Objects?**, p. 82)

  Kazuko-san wa oneesan **ni** nekkuresu o agemashita.
  Kazuko   sister   to   necklace   gave
  *Kazuko gave a necklace **to** her sister.*

- means

  Taitee no hito wa chikatetsu **de** kaisha ni kayoimasu.
  most   of people   subway   by work   to   commute
  *Most people commute to work **by** subway.*

- partner

  Yasuda-san wa okusan **to** joggingu ni ikimashita.
  Mr. Yasuda   wife   with jog   for went
  *Mr. Yasuda went for a jog **with** his wife.*

- purpose

  Yasuda-san wa okusan to joggingu **ni** ikimashita.
  Mr. Yasuda   wife   with jog   for went
  *Mr. Yasuda went **for** a jog with his wife.*

- possession (see **What is the Possessive?**, p. 18)

  kazoku **no** shashin
  family   of   picture
  *the picture **of** my family*

Some complex prepositions in English are expressed by the particle **no** + noun + another particle in Japanese:

no tame ni	*for the purpose of, for the sake of, due to*
no kawari ni	*instead of, in place of, in return for*
no see de	*because of, due to*

Unlike English where the position of the preposition can change in a sentence, Japanese always places particles directly after the noun or pronoun to which they are related. For example, although there are two ways to express the same question in English, there is only one way in Japanese.

> ***Who** are you going out **with**?*
> ***With whom** are you going out?*
> **Dare to** dekakemasu ka.
> who with   are going out

Uses of Prepositions and Particles

Particles, like prepositions, are tricky. Every language uses these functional words differently. Often, when English does not require a preposition, a particle must be used in Japanese. For example, subjects and direct objects do not require prepositions in English, but in Japanese they must be followed by appropriate particles (see **What is a Subject?**, p. 70, and **What are Objects?**, p. 82). These particles enable you to establish the function of the various words in a sentence.

Tomodachi **ga** watashi **ni** kaado **o** kuremashita.
friend | me   to   card | gave

    follows the   follows the   follows the
     subject   indirect obj.   direct obj.

My friend gave me a card.
   subject   indirect obj.   direct obj.

Here are some other differences between English prepositions and Japanese particles.

- some Japanese verbs require a particle while the equivalent English verb does not require a preposition ("x" = noun or pronoun)

No preposition	→	Particle
to marry "x"		"x" **to** kekkon shimasu
to telephone "x"		"x" **ni** denwa o kakemasu
to ask "x"		"x" **ni** kikimasu

- the same preposition is sometimes translated with different particles

Same preposition	→	Different particles
to be in "x"		"x" **ni** imasu
to do in "x"		"x" **de** shimasu
to come from "x"		"x" **kara** kimasu
to differ from "x"		"x" **to** chigaimasu

- different prepostions are sometimes translated with the same particle

Different prepositions →	Same particle
to wait for "x"	"x" **o** machimasu
to listen to "x"	"x" **o** kikimasu

Be sure to memorize Japanese verbs with the appropriate particles.

Particle "No"

A special word needs to be said about the Japanese particle **no** (*'s, of, in, at,* etc.). Its basic function is to link two or more nouns; therefore, it is used in many constructions, such as:

- when a noun possesses another noun, **no** is placed after the possessor (see **What is the Possessive?**, p. 18)

> Mariko-san **no** jitensha
> *Mariko's bicycle*

- when a noun is used to describe another noun, **no** is placed after the noun which describes (see **What is a Descriptive Adjective?**, p. 36)

> konpyuuta **no** sofutowea
> *computer software*

- when expressing the location of someone or something relative to another person, thing, or building, **no** is placed between the noun and the location. Pay attention to the Japanese word order of the location phrase (noun + **no** + location noun) as it is the opposite of the English one (location + noun). Here are some examples.

> Tanaka-san **no ushiro**   →   ***behind*** *Mr. Tanaka*
> Mr. Tanaka's back (the back of Mr. Tanaka)
>
> teeburu **no ue**   →   ***on*** *the table*
> the table's top (the top of the table)
>
> hoteru **no soba**   →   ***close to*** *a hotel*
> a hotel's close place (the close place of a hotel)

▼▼▼▼▼▼▼▼▼▼▼▼▼▼▼▼REVIEW▼▼▼▼▼▼▼▼▼▼▼▼▼▼▼▼

Circle the prepositions in the following sentences.

1. The lecture was about relations among the Pacific Rim countries.

2. The professor came from Osaka last month.

3. The security guards stood beside the gate.

4. I saw a movie at the new theater by the station.

5. The high school I went to had a good tennis team.

6. Here's the person I've been waiting for.

13. WHAT IS A CONJUNCTION?

A **conjunction** is a word that links words or groups of words.

IN ENGLISH
There are two kinds of conjunctions: coordinating and subordinating (see **What are the Different Types of Sentences and Clauses?**, p. 167).

Coordinating conjunctions join words, phrases, and clauses that are equal; they coordinate elements of equal rank. The major coordinating conjunctions are *and, but, or, nor,* and *yet.*

> good *or* evil
> over the river *and* through the woods
> They invited us, *but* we couldn't go.

Subordinating conjunctions join a dependent clause to a main clause; they subordinate one clause to another. A clause introduced by a subordinating conjunction is called a **subordinate clause.** Typical subordinating conjunctions are *before, after, since, although, because, if, unless, so that, while, that,* and *when.*

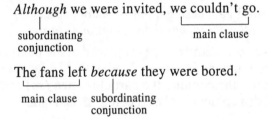

Notice that the subordinate clause may come either before or after the main clause.

IN JAPANESE
As in English, there are coordinating and subordinating conjunctions. They are expressed by two classes of words: conjunctions and conjunctive particles.

Conjunctions are words that show the connection in meaning between a preceding sentence and a following sentence that they introduce. The two sentences connected remain independent grammatically.

> Shiken wa yasashikatta desu. **Dakara**, minna yoku dekimashita.
> └─────── one sentence ───────┘ └─────── another sentence ───────┘
> *The exam was easy. **Therefore**, everyone did well.*

Nihon wa chiisai kuni desu. **Shikashi**, jinkoo wa ooi desu.
*Japan is a small country. **However**, the population is large.*

Conjunctive particles are particles that join nouns or clauses.

- noun + conjunctive particle + noun

Teeburu **to** sofa ga arimasu.
   noun   noun
*There are a table **and** a sofa.*

Koohii **ka** koocha o nomimasu.
*I'll drink coffee **or** tea.*

- clause + conjunctive particle + clause
  In this case the two clauses are connected to form one sentence.

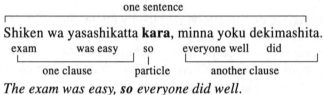

*The exam was easy, **so** everyone did well.*

Nihon wa chiisai kuni desu **ga**, jinkoo wa ooi desu.
*Japan is a small country, **but** the population is large.*

A subordinate clause (i.e., **...kara**, **...ga**) is placed at the beginning of a senyence, preceding a main clause. Notice that in Japanese a comma is inserted after the conjunctive particles **kara** *(so)* and **ga** *(but)*, while in English a comma is placed before *so* and *but*.

Rather than using a separate word or particle, the most common way to join clauses and express the meaning "and" in Japanese is to use the **te** form of verbs, of the copula, or of **i**-type adjectives (see p. 168).

Watashi ga ryoori o **shite**, ruumumeeto ga sara o araimasu.
  I   cooking do-and roommate   dishes   washes
               te form of the verb **suru** *(to do)*
*I **do** the cooking, **and** my roommate washes the dishes.*

Careful

Some English conjunctions, such as *when* and *after*, are translated into Japanese by a noun + a particle, such as **toki** *(time)* + **ni** and **ato** *(time* *after)* + **de**. These nouns, **toki** and **ato** are modified by a relative clause (see **What is a Relative Clause?**, p. 177). Since the particles are optional, they appear in parentheses below.

Nihonjin wa gohan o taberu **toki** (**ni**), hashi o tsukaimasu.
Japanese   meal   eat   time at chopsticks   use
*Japanese use chopsticks **when** they eat a meal.*

Kaimono o shita **ato** (**de**), eega o mimashita.
shopping did after at movie   saw
*I saw a movie **after** I did my shopping.*

▼▼▼▼▼▼▼▼▼▼▼▼▼▼▼▼REVIEW▼▼▼▼▼▼▼▼▼▼▼▼▼▼▼▼

Circle the coordinating and subordinating conjunctions in the following sentences.
▪ Underline the words or groups of words which each conjunction serves to coordinate or to subordinate.

1. Yoshiko and Mami are going to Boston or New York.

2. I did my homework, but my dog ate it.

3. Mr. Tanaka has to borrow money so he can buy a car.

4. My friend is supposed to call me when she gets home.

14. WHAT IS AN INTERJECTION?

An **interjection** is a word that expresses an abrupt emotion, calls out or responds to someone. It usually appears at the beginning of a sentence and stands apart from the grammar of the sentence.

IN ENGLISH

There are a great variety of such words, including most words of swearing and profanity. They belong to both written and spoken language, but more often to the latter. An interjection is separated from the main clause by a comma and the sentence often ends with an exclamation mark.

> *Oh,* how beautiful it is!
> *Wow*, we did it!
> *Hey*, you!
> *Huh*?

IN JAPANESE

A similar variety of interjections exists in Japanese, expressing awe, surprise, anger, etc., but relatively few words of swearing and profanity. Japanese people speak differently in informal and formal situations (see **What is Meant by Polite and Plain Forms?**, p. 57) and many of the interjections are used in informal situations only. Also, some interjections are used strictly by men, some strictly by women, and others by both.

	Oh, how beautiful it is!
formal male speech	**Aa**, kiree desu nee.
formal female speech	**Aa** (*or* **Ara**, **Maa**), kiree desu nee.
informal male speech	**Aa**, kiree da naa.
informal female speech	**Aa** (*or* **Ara**, **Maa**), kiree nee.
	Wow, we did it!
informal male speech	**Waa** (*or* **Oo**), yatta zo.
informal female speech	**Waa**, yatta wa nee.
	Hey, you!
informal male speech	**Oi** (*or* **Yoo**), chotto.
informal female speech	**Nee**, chotto.
	Huh?
formal male and female speech	**Hai**?
informal male and female speech	**E**? *or* **N**?

15. WHAT ARE PREFIXES AND SUFFIXES?

A **prefix** is a short element attached to the beginning of a word or stem to change its meaning or to add additional meaning. A prefix is not a word; therefore, it cannot be used by itself.

common **un**common
national **inter**national

A **suffix** is a short element attached to the end of a word or stem to change that word into a different part of speech or to form an inflectional ending. A suffix is not a word; therefore, it cannot be used by itself. (See **What is Meant by Inflection?**, p. 59, **What is Meant by the Inflection of a Verb?**, p. 61, **What is Meant by the Inflection of the Verb "To be"?**, p. 65, and **What is Meant by the Inflection of an Adjective?**, p. 68).

adjective	→ **noun**	gentle	→ gentle**ness**
verb	→ **adjective**	love	→ love**able**
singular noun	→ **plural noun**	book	→ book**s**
verb present tense	→ **verb past tense**	delay	→ delay**ed**

To see how prefixes and suffixes work, let us look at various English verbs that come from the Latin verb **duco** *(to lead)*. Different prefixes give us the verbs *induce, deduce, reduce, seduce, produce, introduce, adduce, educe*. With suffixes we can create different parts of speech, for example, *induction* (noun), *inductive* (adjective), *inductively* (adverb), and indicate inflections such as *induces* (present tense with a third person singular subject) and *induced* (past tense). For a discussion of "person" and "singular-plural," see **What is a Personal Pronoun?**, p. 10, and **What is Meant by Number?**, p. 13.

IN ENGLISH
Many of our prefixes and suffixes come from Latin and Greek. A good English dictionary will tell you the meanings and functions of the various prefixes and suffixes. Knowing the meaning of prefixes can help you increase your English vocabulary.

anti- (against)	+ body	→	**anti**body
sub- (under)	+ marine	→	**sub**marine
mal- (bad)	+ nutrition	→	**mal**nutrition

Likewise, knowing suffixes can help you increase your vocabulary and also identify the parts of speech in a sentence.

-able/-ible	toler**able**	→	**adjective**
-ence/-ance	reli**ance**	→	**noun**
-en	cheap**en**	→	**verb**

IN JAPANESE

Prefixes, and especially suffixes, play an important role in Japanese. Suffixes are the basis of inflections indicating negation and tense, among others, and they can also change words from one part of speech to another (see **What are Affirmative and Negative Sentences?**, p. 92, and **What is Meant by Tense?**, p. 132). As in English, knowing the meaning of prefixes and suffixes will help you increase your Japanese vocabulary and help you identify parts of speech.

The prefixes and suffixes that are of a Japanese native origin are usually attached to native Japanese words. The prefixes and suffixes that are of Chinese origin are usually attached to words borrowed from Chinese.

PREFIXES—Here are examples of prefixes in Japanese.

- to make an expression polite: **o-** + noun

sara	*dishes*	→	**o**sara	*dishes*

- to intensify *(truly...)*: **ma-** + adjective stem

kura-	*dark*	→	**ma**kkura	*pitch dark*

- to negate *(un-/in-)*: **fu-** + adjective of Chinese origin

tekitoo	*appropriate*	→	**fu**tekitoo	*inappropriate*

- to refer to previous *(ex-, former)*: **zen-** + noun of Chinese origin

daitooryoo	*president*	→	**zen**daitooryoo	*former president*

SUFFIXES—Here are examples of suffixes in Japanese.

Various forms of verbs:

- **ru** verb stem + **-ta**: past tense form

oki-	*wake up*	→	oki**ta**	*woke up*

- **ru** verb stem + **-rareru**: passive form

tate-	*build*	→	tate**rareru**	*be built*

- **u** verb stem + **-e**: imperative form

ik-	*go*	→	ik**e**	*Go!*

Some suffixes change the parts of speech of the word to which they are attached, while others do not.

- to address someone politely: noun + **-san**

  Yamada *surname* → Yamada-**san** *Mr. (Ms.) Yamada*

- to count bound objects: number + **-satsu** (see p.14)

  ni *two* → ni-**satsu** *two books, notebooks*

- to add the meaning "*-ization*": noun of Chinese origin + **-ka**

  kindai *modern times* → kindai**ka** *modernization*

- to turn adjective into a noun: adjective stem + **-sa**

  naga- *long* → naga**sa** *length*

- to turn verb into an adjective *(easy to...)*: verb (stem of **masu** form) + **-yasui**

  yomi- *read* → yomi**yasui** *easy to read*

It is important to know that some independent words in English will be expressed by suffixes in Japanese.

- to express the ability to do something *(can, able to)*: **u** verb stem + **-eru**

  kak- *write* → kak**eru** *can write*

- to express the causative (to make someone do something): **u** verb stem + **-aseru** (see **What is the Causative Construction?**, p. 161)

  kak- *write* → kak**aseru** *make (someone) write*

- to express *to seem, to look*: verb or adjective stem + **-soo**

  furi- *rain* → furi**soo** *seem like rain*
  taka- *expensive* → taka**soo** *look expensive*

▼▼▼▼▼▼▼▼▼▼▼▼▼▼▼▼▼REVIEW▼▼▼▼▼▼▼▼▼▼▼▼▼▼▼▼▼

I. Underline the prefixes in the following words.

1. uncertain
2. enlarge
3. misunderstand
4. repay
5. decode

II. Underline the suffixes in the following words.

1. graceful
2. sleepless
3. worker
4. shorten
5. depends

16. WHAT IS MEANT BY POLITE AND PLAIN FORMS?

Whatever the language, people vary their speaking styles according to the situation. For example, when speaking to a boss or professor in a formal setting, we use a more formal and polite style than when we speak to our friends at a party.

IN ENGLISH
Variations in speaking styles exist in English:

> Open the door!
> Please open the door.
> Will you open the door?
> I would be most obliged if you would kindly open the door.

These variations, however, are not grammatical changes; rather, they are a matter of different levels of politeness reflecting the personal choice of the speaker. In other words, there is no grammatical construction in English that requires one style over the other.

IN JAPANESE
In Japanese the distinction between styles is not always a matter of personal choice; it is often mandated by grammar. There are two styles in Japanese, the **polite** style, which is more formal, and the **plain** style. All the verbs, the copula *(to be)*, and **i**-type adjectives have a plain and a polite form, both expressing the same meaning.

	Polite form	Plain form	
verb	mimasu	miru	*see*
copula	desu	da	*be, am, is, are*
i-type adjective	samui desu	samui	*is cold*

As in English, one style, rather than the other, is chosen by the speaker according to the situation. You will use the polite form if you are talking to someone you do not know well or someone older than you to whom you must show respect (i.e., your teacher, your friend's parents), and the plain form if you are talking to a close friend in an informal setting.

Although there are differences between male and female speech in the polite style, the differences are more numerous and prominent in the plain style. For example, men and women use different sets of vocabulary (for instance, the equivalent of the pronoun "I" is **boku** for men and **atashi** for women) and the particle attached to the end of a sentence is used differently by men and women. The copula **da** is omitted in female speech while it is retained in male speech. Also, when speaking in the plain style, both men and women often omit particles such as **wa**, **o**, and **e** attached to nouns, as well as other elements of a sentence. When you learn to speak in the plain style, you must understand the totality of the way the language is used.

To give you an idea of the difference between the two styles, here are some examples of an English sentence expressed in both the plain style and polite style in Japanese. The particles that appear in parentheses below are usually omitted.

POLITE STYLE
male and female speech   **Watashi wa** ashita Oosaka e **ikimasu**.
                             I   tomorrow Osaka to will go

PLAIN STYLE
male speech   **Boku (wa)** ashita Oosaka **(e) iku yo**.
female speech   **Atashi (wa)** ashita Oosaka **(e) iku no yo**.
                             I'll go to Osaka tomorrow.

POLITE STYLE
male and female speech   Are wa atarashii roketto **desu ne**.
                             that   new   rocket   is

PLAIN STYLE
male speech   Are (wa) atarashii roketto **da ne**.
female speech   Are (wa) atarashii roketto **ne**.
                             That's a new rocket, isn't it?

Certain grammatical constructions, such as a relative clause, require the use of plain style forms (see **What is a Relative Clause?**, p. 177).

Tenisu **o suru** hito wa Honda-san desu.
|‾‾‾‾‾‾‾‾‾‾‾|
 relative clause

   The plain form **suru** *(play)* must be used because it appears within a relative clause.
*The person who **plays** tennis is Ms. Honda.*
          |‾‾‾‾‾‾‾‾‾‾‾‾|
           relative clause

For a discussion of the forms of the polite and plain style of verbs, copula, and **i**-type adjectives see the chapters on the inflection of these parts of speech.

17. WHAT IS MEANT BY INFLECTION?

An **inflection** is a change in the form of a word.

Here are some terms used to talk about inflection:

DICTIONARY FORM—The dictionary form, the form under which a verb appears in the dictionary, is the basic form of a word; as such it is not inflected. For example, *deceive* is the dictionary form of the verb *to deceive*, as opposed to *deceived*, which is an inflected form.

STEM—A **stem** is the part of a word to which prefixes and suffixes can be added (see **What are Prefixes and Suffixes?**, p. 53). For example, *decept-* is a stem, to which suffixes such as *-ion* or *-ive* can be attached to form a noun, *deception*, and an adjective, *deceptive*. A stem rarely changes its form.

IN ENGLISH

Here are some examples of inflection in English.

NOUN—A noun can be inflected:

- to show number, that is, if it refers to one person or thing or to more than one person or thing (see **What is Meant by Number?**, p. 13): singular → *book*; plural → *books*
- to show possession, that is, that the noun is the possessor of something or someone (see **What is the Possessive?**, p. 18): *the president's staff, Amy's car*

PRONOUN—A pronoun can be inflected:

- to show number, that is, if it refers to one person or thing or to more than one person or thing (see **What is a Personal Pronoun?**, p. 10): singular → *I*; plural → *we*
- to show function, that is, the role it plays in a sentence (see **What is a Subject?**, p. 70, and **What are Objects?**, p. 82): subject → *He looks at the mountain*; object → *Everyone looks at him*.

VERB—A verb can be inflected:

- to show person, that is, who or what is performing the action of the verb (see **What is a Personal Pronoun?**, p. 10): first person singular → *I walk*, third person singular → *John walks*
- to show tense, that is, when the action of the verb is taking place (see **What is Meant by Tense?**, p. 132): present → *I walk*; past → *I walked*

- to show voice, that is, the relationship between the subject and the verb (see **What is Meant by Active and Passive Voice?**, p. 153): active → *John sells*; passive → *the ticket is sold*

ADJECTIVE—An adjective can be inflected:

- to show comparison, that is, the degree of a quality (**What is a Descriptive Adjective?**, p. 36): basic → *Mary is lucky*; comparative → *Mary is luckier*; superlative → *Mary is the luckiest*.

IN JAPANESE
There are three parts of speech that are inflected: verbs, the copula *(to be)*, and i-type adjectives. Each one is discussed under a separate chapter (see **What is Meant by the Inflection of a Verb?**, p. 61, **What is Meant by the Inflection of the Verb "To be"?**, p. 65, and **What is Meant by the Inflection of an Adjective?**, p. 68).

18. WHAT IS MEANT BY THE INFLECTION OF A VERB?

A verb changes form to show various factors, such as person, tense and voice in English, and style, tense, and affirmative-negative in Japanese. This change of form is called **inflection** (see **What is Meant by Inflection?**, p. 59).

IN ENGLISH
English verbs can be affected by various factors:

- the person or thing doing the action (see **What is a Personal Pronoun?**, p. 10)

  first person singular → I *am*
  third person singular → he *is*

- the number of persons or things doing the action

  first person **singular** → I *am*
  first person **plural** → we *are*

- the tense, that is, the period of time when the action takes place (see **What is Meant by Tense?**, p. 132)

  present → I *study*
  past → I *studied*

- whether the subject of the verb is the doer of the action, i.e., the active voice, or the receiver of the action, i.e., passive voice (see **What is Meant by Active and Passive Voice?**, p. 153).

  active → John *invites* his Japanese friends.
  passive → John *is invited.*

Nevertheless, English verbs change relatively little. Let us look at the forms of the verb *to write.*

1. **dictionary form**	**write**	
imperative	write	*Write!*
present tense	write	I, you, we, they *write.*
2. **3rd person singular**		
present tense	**writes**	He, she, it *writes.*
3. **past tense**	**wrote**	I *wrote.*
4. **present participle**	**writing**	I am *writing.*
5. **past participle**	**written**	I have *written.*

As you can see, this verb has only five different forms. These forms are discussed in the chapters devoted to various tenses. (See **What is the Imperative?**, p. 150, **What is the Present Tense?**, p. 136, **What is the Past Tense?**, p. 142).

IN JAPANESE

Verb forms change constantly. Unlike English verbs, however, Japanese verbs are not affected by person or number. Notice in the following two sentences that there is no difference in the verb form, in spite of the fact that the person doing the action changes from the first person to the third person singular.

> Watashi wa **arukimasu**.
> 1st person singular
> *I walk.*

> Michiko-san wa **arukimasu**.
> 3rd person singular
> *Michiko walks.*

Most forms of a Japanese verb reflect the following three features: style, tense, and the affirmative-negative distinction.

STYLE—The verb can be either in the plain or the polite form. The polite form of a verb is also called the **"masu** form." (See **What is Meant by Polite and Plain Forms?**, p. 57.)

TENSE—The verb can be in the nonpast or the past form: ex. *go, will go* (nonpast) and *went* (past). (See **What is Meant by Tense?**, p. 132.)

AFFIRMATIVE-NEGATIVE DISTINCTION—The verb can be either in the affirmative or negative form: ex. *go* (affirmative) and *not go* (negative). (See **What Are Affirmative and Negative Sentences?**, p. 92.)

The basic form of the verb is the plain, nonpast, affirmative form. It is called the **dictionary form** because it is under this form that it is entered in a dictionary.

There are many factors to consider when selecting the proper form of a verb in Japanese. To make sure that you understand each factor, study the chapters in this handbook where they are discussed, as well as the more detailed explanations in your textbook.[1]

Examples of the Inflection of Japanese Verbs

All Japanese verbs end with the sound **-u** in the dictionary form and are classified as either regular or irregular verbs. There are only two irregular verbs, **kuru** *(come),* and **suru** *(do).* Regular verbs are further

---

[1]Most of the features and forms discussed in this chapter apply to the three parts of speech that can function as a main predicate in Japanese: verbs, the copula and i-type adjectives (see pp. 65 and 68). Note that the **ba** form does not have tense or style, the **oo** form does not make the affirmative-negative distinction, and the **te** form does not have tense.

classifed as either **ru** verbs or **u** verbs. Changes in the verb form are achieved through the use of suffixes attached to the stem of the verb (see **What are Prefixes and Suffixes?**, p. 53).

STEM—Let us first see how to find the stem of a verb. The stem of an **u** verb is obtained by deleting the **u** at the end of the dictionary form and the stem of a **ru** verb by deleting the **ru**.

	u verb		ru verb	
dictionary form	kak**u**	*to write*	tabe**ru**	*to eat*
stem	kak-		tabe-	

FORMS OF **U** VERB—The various forms of the **u** verbs are obtained by the stem + appropriate vowels + appropriate suffixes. The **u** verbs are sometimes called **five-row verbs** because they are conjugated on five rows of the Japanese alphabet chart: **a, i, u, e, o**.

a → precedes the negative suffix **-nai**
i → precedes the polite suffix **-masu**
u → indicates the plain nonpast affirmative form
e → makes a verb form called the **ba** form, meaning *"if"*
  (see **What is a Conditional Clause?**, p. 174)
o → makes a verb form called the **oo** form, meaning *"I shall do..."* or *"let's do... ."*

The **te** form, which is used to link a verb to another main predicate (see p. 168), and the plain past affirmative form of **u** verbs follow different patterns depending on the last syllable of their dictionary forms: ex. kak**u** → ka**ite**, ka**ita**; hana**su** → hana**shite**, hana**shita**; yo**mu** → yo**nde**, yo**nda**. Consult your textbook.

For example, look at some of the forms of the verb **kaku** *(to write)*, below (the vowel added in to each stem is indicated in ***bold italic*** and the suffix in **bold**).

STEM	kak-	*write*
plain nonpast negative (**-*a*-nai**)	kak*a***nai**	*not write*
polite form (**-*i*-masu**)	kak*i***masu**	*write*
dictionary form		
= plain nonpast affirmative (**-*u***)	kak*u*	*write*
ba form (**-*e*-ba**)	kak*e***ba**	*if (you) write*
oo form (**-*o*-o**)	kak*o***o**	*I shall write, let's write*
te form	ka**ite**	*write and*
plain past affirmative form	ka**ita**	*wrote*

FORMS OF **RU** VERB—The inflection of the **ru** verbs is much simpler than that of the **u** verbs. The **ru** verbs are sometimes called **one-row verbs** because the same vowel at the end of the stem appears for all forms.

STEM	m*i*-	*see*
dictionary form =		
plain nonpast affirmative form	m*i***ru**	*see*
plain nonpast negative form	m*i***nai**	*not see*
polite form	m*i***masu**	*see*
ba form	m*i***reba**	*if (you) see*
oo form	m*i***yoo**	*I shall see, Let's see*
te form	m*i***te**	*see and*
plain past affirmative form	m*i***ta**	*saw*
STEM	tab*e*-	*eat*
dictionary form =		
plain nonpast affirmative form	tab*e***ru**	*eat*
plain nonpast negative form	tab*e***nai**	*not eat*
polite form	tab*e***masu**	*eat*
ba form	tab*e***rba**	*if (you) eat*
oo form	tab*e***yoo**	*I shall eat, Let's eat*
te form	tab*e***te**	*eat and*
plain past affirmative form	tab*e***ta**	*ate*

The inflection of the two irregular verbs must be memorized separately.

19. WHAT IS MEANT BY THE INFLECTION OF THE VERB "TO BE"?

The verb *to be*, like other verbs, changes form to indicate things such as person, tense and voice. This change of forms is called **inflection**.

IN ENGLISH

The verb *to be* is used with nouns, adjectives and prepositional phrases (see **What are the Uses of the Verb "To be"?**, p. 26). It is a special kind of verb that changes more than other verbs.

dictionary form	be	
imperative	be	*Be nice!*
present participle	being	*He is being nice.*
past participle	been	*He has been nice.*

PRESENT TENSE

1st person singular	am	*I am healthy.*
1st person plural	are	*We are healthy.*
2nd person singular	are	*You are healthy.*
2nd person plural	are	*You are healthy.*
3rd person singular	is	*He, she, it is healthy.*
3rd person plural	are	*They are healthy.*

PAST TENSE

1st person singular	was	*I was healthy.*
1st person plural	were	*We were healthy.*
2nd person singular	were	*You were healthy.*
2nd person plural	were	*You were healthy.*
3rd person singular	was	*He, she, it was healthy.*
3rd person plural	were	*They were healthy.*

IN JAPANESE

The Japanese equivalent of the verb *to be* is called the **copula**. The copula is a part of speech in its own right and serves as a main predicate in a sentence (see p. 81). It is attached to nouns and to the stem of one type of adjectives called **na**-type adjectives (see p. 37). Unlike English, it is not affected by number or person. However, as all main predicates in Japanese, the copula changes according to style, tense, and the affirmative-negative distinction (see p. 62).

Let us look at various forms of the copula attached to the noun **isha** *(doctor)* and to the **na**-type adjective stem **genki** *(healthy)*. The forms 1-5 below are given in the polite style (forms 6 and 7 do no have the polite or plain style).

COPULA WITH NOUN

1. nonpast affirmative	isha **desu**	*is a doctor*
2. nonpast negative	isha **dewa arimasen**	*is not a doctor*
3. past affirmative	isha **deshita**	*was a doctor*
4. past negative	isha **dewa arimasendeshita**	*was not a doctor*
5. **te** form	isha **de**	*is a doctor and*
6. **ba** form	isha **nara(ba)**	*if (s/he) is a doctor*
7. attributive form	isha **no** (kodomo)	*doctor's (child)*

COPULA WITH **NA**-TYPE ADJECTIVE

1. nonpast affirmative	genki **desu**	*is healthy*
2. nonpast negative	genki **dewa arimasen**	*is not healthy*
3. past affirmative	genki **deshita**	*was healthy*
4. past negative	genki **dewa arimasendeshita**	*was not healthy*
5. **te** form	genki **de**	*is healthy and*
6. **ba** form	genki **nara(ba)**	*if (s/he) is healthy*
7. attributive form	genki **na** (kodomo)	healthy (child)

As you can see, the forms of the copula are the same whether they are attached to a noun or to a **na**-type adjective stem. The only exception is in the attributive form: **no** is used when a noun modifies another noun, while **na** is used when a **na**-type adjective modifies a noun (hence the name "**na**-type"). By memorizing the above patterns, you can use the appropriate form with any noun and **na**-type adjective stem.

Note that **dewa** used in the negative forms is often shortened to **ja**.

Isha **ja** arimasen.
　　dewa
She (or he) is not a doctor.

Genki **ja** arimasendeshita.
　　dewa
She (or he) was not healthy.

Here are some examples of the use of the various forms of the copula. Suppose that you are talking politely to your Japanese friend's mother.

My brother is an engineer.
　　1. Polite or plain? → polite
　　2. Tense? → nonpast
　　3. Affirmative or negative? → affirmative

Ani wa gishi **desu**.
polite affirmative in nonpast

*My father **was not** an engineer.*
1. Polite or plain? → polite
2. Tense? → past
3. Affirmative or negative? → negative

Chichi wa gishi **dewa (ja) arimasendeshita**.
                        |
                 polite negative in past

20. WHAT IS MEANT BY THE INFLECTION OF AN ADJECTIVE?

An adjective can change form to reflect other characteristics besides the meaning of the adjective itself. This change of form is called **inflection**.

IN ENGLISH

The only inflected forms of English adjectives are the **comparative** and **superlative** forms. Let us look at these two forms of the adjective *happy*.

comparative form	happi**er**
superlative form	happi**est**

IN JAPANESE

Of the two types of adjectives, namely the **i**-type adjectives are inflected (see p. 37 in **What is a Descriptive Adjective?**). As all main predicates in Japanese, they change according to the style, tense, and affirmative-negative distinction (see p. 62).

The various forms of the **i**-type adjectives are composed of a stem + a suffix. The stem of an **i**-type adjective is obtained by deleting the last sound "i".

dictionary form	atsu**i**	*hot*
stem	atsu-	

Let us look at various forms of the **i**-type adjective **atsui** *(hot)*. The forms 1-5 below are given in the polite style (forms 6 and 7 do not have the polite or plain style).

1. nonpast affirmative	atsu**i desu**	*is hot*
2. nonpast negative	atsu**ku arimasen**	*is not hot*
3. past affirmative	atsu**katta desu**	*was hot*
4. past negative	atsu**ku arimasendeshita**	*was not hot*
5. **te** form	atsu**kute**	*is hot and*
6. **ba** form	atsu**kereba**	*if (it) is hot*
7. attributive form	atsu**i** (hi)	*hot (day)*

As almost all **i**-type adjectives follow this regular pattern, only one example must be memorized and the pattern can then be applied to others.

The **te** form is used to link an adjective to another adjective, to a verb or to a clause (see **What are the Different Types of Sentences and Clauses?**, p. 167).

> Kyoo wa **atsukute**, harete imasu.
> today   is hot and   sunny   is
> |
>   **te** form
> *Today **is hot and** sunny.*

The **ba** form is used to express a condition under which the clause that follows will be true (see **What is a Conditional Clause?**, p. 174).

> Ashita wa **atsukereba**, oyogi ni ikimasu.
> tomorrow   if it is hot   swim   for   will go
> |
>   **ba** form
> ***If it is hot** tomorrow, I'll go for a swim.*

The attributive form is used to modify a noun (see **What is a Descriptive Adjective?**, p. 36).

> **Atsui** hi ni wa mizu o takusan nomimasu.
> hot   day on   water   a lot   drink
> | |
> | noun modified
> attributive form
> *On **hot** days I drink a lot of water.*

Unlike English, Japanese adjectives do not have a comparative or superlative forms.

21. WHAT IS A SUBJECT?

In a sentence describing an action, the person or thing that performs the action is called the **subject**.[1] When you wish to find the subject of the sentence, look for the verb first; then ask, *who?* or *what?* before the verb. The answer will be the subject.

Mr. Brown speaks Japanese.

> *Who* speaks Japanese?
> Answer: Mr. Brown.
> *Mr. Brown* is the subject.

The trees fell to the ground.

> *What* fell to the ground?
> Answer: the trees.
> *Trees* is the subject.

In a sentence describing a state of affairs, the person or thing that is characterized as being in that state is the **subject**. To find the subject of the sentence, ask *who is?* or *what is?* before the adjective or noun. The answer will be the subject.

Mr. Brown is a businessman.

> *Who is* a businessman?
> Answer: Mr. Brown.
> *Mr. Brown* is the subject.

The trees are tall.

> *What is* tall?
> Answer: the trees.
> *Trees* is the subject.

A subject is often longer than just one word. The method of identifying a longer subject is exactly the same as the one used to identify a single word subject. To find these longer subjects, you must learn to identify a group of words that go together by meaning.

All the new Cabinet members gathered together.
|_____|
            subject

> *Who* gathered?
> Answer: All the new Cabinet members.
> *All the new Cabinet members* as a group is the subject.

---

[1]The subject performs the action in an active sentence, but is acted upon in a passive sentence (see **What is Meant by Active and Passive Voice?**, p. 153).

People who can speak Japanese are in great demand.
└──────────────────────┘
       subject

Who are in great demand?
Answer: People who can speak Japanese.
People who can speak Japanese as a group is the subject.

In a sentence such as the one below, "Hiroshi and Yuko" counts as one subject, and not two, because that entire phrase can be replaced by the pronoun *they*.

Hiroshi and Yuko play tennis two hours every day.
└──────────────┘
     subject

They play tennis two hours every day.
│
subject → *Hiroshi and Yuko*

On the other hand, some sentences have more than one verb; in that case, you have to find the subject of each verb by asking the *who?* question before each verb.

    The president issued an order and **his staff** carried it out.
      Who issued an order?
      Answer: The president → *the president* is the subject of *issued*.
      Who carried it out?
      Answer: His staff → *his staff* is the subject of *carried it out*.

    The computer is expensive, but **the printer** is on sale.
      What is expensive?
      Answer: The computer → *the computer* is the subject of *is expensive*.
      What is on sale?
      Answer: The printer → *the printer* is the subject of *is on sale*.

Train yourself to ask the appropriate questions to find the subject. Never assume a word is the subject because it comes first in the sentence. Subjects can be located in various places, as you can see in the following examples where the subject is in **bold italic** and the verb in plain *italic*:

    *Did **the game** start on time?*
    After singing karaoke for two hours, ***George** became* exhausted.
    Looking in the mirror *was **a little girl***.

In both English and Japanese it is important to identify the subject of each main predicate in order to understand the sentence correctly. In Japanese the copula and i-type adjectives, in addition to verbs, take a subject (see **What is a Predicate?**, p. 79).

▼▼▼▼▼▼▼▼▼▼▼▼▼▼▼▼▼▼**REVIEW**▼▼▼▼▼▼▼▼▼▼▼▼▼▼▼▼▼▼▼

Find the subjects in the following sentences.
- Next to Q, write the question you need to ask to find the subject.
- Next to A, write the answer to the question you just asked.

1. When the band started playing music, all the players came out.

Q: _____

A: _____

Q: _____

A: _____

2. One waiter took the order, another waiter brought the food.

Q: _____

A: _____

Q: _____

A: _____

3. The students voted for the class president.

Q: _____

A: _____

4. My mother is always right.

Q: _____

A: _____

5. Difficult as it may be, Japanese is an interesting language.

Q: _____

A: _____

Q: _____

A: _____

22. WHAT IS A TOPIC?

A **topic** in the grammatical sense is the element of a sentence which expresses what the sentence is about. It can be one word or a group of words. The rest of the sentence is called a **comment**, that is, information about the topic.

Meat, I don't eat.
  topic   comment

To Chicago, I suggest you take the train.
    topic   comment

The topic of a sentence is a piece of information that is shared between the speaker and the listener. For example, the first sentence above could be in response to a question that has been asked, implicitly or explicitly, by the listener about "meat" and the second about "how to get to Chicago."

The topic of a sentence must be distinguished from the topic of a conversation. For instance, the topic of a conversation can be a certain movie, but the topic of each sentence about the movie can vary as shown below.

Yesterday my wife and I saw an interesting movie.
topic of this sentence

I thought the acting was great.
topic of this sentence

The cinematography was also superb.
topic of this sentence

IN ENGLISH

The topic is usually the first noun or phrase in a sentence. Since the subject often appears at the beginning of a sentence (see **What is a Subject?**, p. 70), the subject and the topic are very often the same word. However, just as you cannot assume that the first word in a sentence is the subject, you cannot assume that the subject is always the topic.

In the sentence below, the topic and the subject of the sentence are not the same.

Salads, I love; *sweets, I* avoid.
   | | | |
topic subject   topic subject

> *Salads* is the topic of the first sentence because it is about salads.
> *Sweets* is the topic of the second sentence because it is about sweets.
> *I* is the subject of both sentences because it is the performer of the
> verb *love* and *avoid*.

The topic of a sentence can be a word performing a variety of functions in a sentence. Here are some examples (the word in *italics* is the subject of the sentence, the one in **bold** is the topic).

▪ subject

> ***Kazuko*** gave Akira a tie.
>
> Possibly an answer to the question: "What did **Kazuko** do?".
> You are talking about what **Kazuko**, as opposed to what anyone
> else did, so **Kazuko** is the topic.

▪ direct object (see **What are Objects?**, p. 82)

> **The tie**, *Kazuko* gave it to Akira yesterday.
>
> Possibly an answer to the question: "Whom did Kazuko give
> **the tie** to?" or "What happened to **the tie**?"
> You are talking about what happened to **the tie**, as opposed to
> any other object, so **the tie** is the topic.

▪ indirect object

> **To Akira**, *Kazuko* gave a tie yesterday.
>
> Possibly an answer to the question: "What did Kazuko give **to
> Akira**?"
> You are talking about what was given **to Akira**, as opposed to
> what was given to anyone else, so **to Akira** is the topic.

▪ time

> **Yesterday**, *Kazuko* gave Akira a tie.
>
> Possibly an answer to the question: "What happened **yes-
> terday**?" or "What did Kazuko give to Akira **yesterday**?"
> You are talking about what happened **yesterday**, as opposed to
> any other day, so **yesterday** is the topic.

▪ place

> **At the party,** *Kazuko* gave Akira a tie.
>> Possibly an answer to the question: "What happened **at the party**?"
>> You are talking about what happened **at the party**, as opposed to anywhere else, so **at the party** is the topic .

We sometimes use the phrases *as for*, *speaking of*, and the like, to express a topic in English.

> *As for the **software*** just mentioned, we have a great interest in it.
> *Speaking of the test*, I have some questions.

One important thing to remember about the difference between a topic and a subject is that none of the interrogative words, such as *who* or *what*, can be a topic, though they can be a subject (see **What is an Interrogative Word?**, p. 102).

For example, you can transform "Is Mr. Oda going to the concert?" into "As for Mr. Oda, is he going to the concert?" with "Mr. Oda" as the topic. However, you cannot transform "Who is going to the concert?" into "As for whom, is he going to the concert?" because you cannot talk about an undefined "whom."

To decide whether a word in a specific sentence is a subject or a topic, you may find it helpful to look at the question the sentence is answering, or if there is no stated question, to ask yourself what question it could be answering. In example 1, the commonly shared noun, *Mr. Oda*, is the topic. In example 2, the newly presented noun, *Mr. Oda* is not.

1. **question**   What will *Mr. Oda* do?
                                        |
                                subject and topic

   answer   *Mr. Oda* will go to the concert.
                            |
                    subject and topic

2. **question**   *Who* will go to the concert?
                        |
                subject, but not topic

   answer   *Mr. Oda* will go to the concert.
                            |
                    subject, but not topic

IN JAPANESE

Just as in English, a topic is usually the first noun or phrase in a sentence, and the subject of a sentence often coincides with the topic of the same sentence. It is important to distinguish a subject functioning as topic from a plain subject because each one will be marked with a different particle. A subject functioning as a topic is marked with the particle **wa**, while a plain subject is marked with the particle **ga**.[1]

When deciding which particle is appropriate, **wa** or **ga**, you should always use the same particle in your answer as the one in the question. If there is no stated question, ask yourself what question it could be answering.

1. **question**   *What will **Mr.Oda** do?*
    Oda-san *wa* nani o shimasu ka.
    |
    subject and topic

   answer   *Mr. Oda will go to the concert.*
    Oda-san *wa* konsaato e ikimasu.
    |
    subject and topic

As in English, an interrogative word can function as a subject, but not as a topic; in other words, an interrogative word can only take the particle **ga**, but never **wa**. Since the same particle must be used in the answer as the one in the question, the answer to a question containing *who, what,* etc. as the subject will always have a subject followed by the particle **ga**.

2. **question**   *Who will go to the concert?*
    Dare *ga* konsaato e ikimasu ka.
    |
    subject, but not topic

   answer   *Mr. Oda will go to the concert.*
    Oda-san *ga* konsaato e ikimasu.
    |
    subject, but not topic

The use of the particles **wa** and **ga** to distinguish topics from subjects in Japanese can be compared to the use of vocal emphasis in English.

---

[1] In casual conversation, however, the particle **wa** is often omitted.

For instance, when answering the first question "What will Mr. Oda do?" you will say "Mr. Oda will go to the concert" with stress on "to the concert." On the other hand, when answering the second question "Who will go to the concert?" you will stress "Mr. Oda."

When a subject or a direct object in a sentence is identified as a topic, the particle **ga** indicating the function of subject and the particle **o** indicating direct object are replaced by **wa**.

- when the topic is a subject → **wa** replaces **ga**

   Kazuko-san *wa* kinoo Akira-san ni nekutai o agemashita.

   replaces the original particle **ga** which follows a subject

   Kazuko gave Akira a tie yesterday.

- when the topic is a direct object → **wa** replaces **o**

   Nekutai *wa* Kazuko-san ga kinoo Akira-san ni agemashita.

   replaces the original particle **o** which follows a direct object

   The tie, Kazuko gave it to Akira yesterday.

Particles indicating a grammatical function other than subject and direct object are usually retained and the particle **wa** added.

- when the topic is an indirect object → **wa** is added to **ni**

   Akira-san ni *wa* Kazuko-san ga kinoo nekutai o agemashita.

   wa is added to the particle **ni** which follows an indirect object

   To Akira, Kazuko gave a tie yesterday.

- when the topic is time → **wa** is added to the time word (or to **ni**, if stated)

   Kinoo *wa* Kazuko-san ga Akira-san ni nekutai o agemashita.

   wa is added (**kinoo** does not take a particle when it is not a topic)

   Yesterday, Kazuko gave Akira a tie.

- when the topic is place → **wa** is added to the particle **de** or **ni**

   Paatii de *wa* Kazuko-san ga Akira-san ni nekutai o agemashita.

   wa is added to the particle **de** which follows a place

   At the party, Kazuko gave Akira a tie.

There is a special sentence structure with both a topic and a subject in Japanese, to which there is no corresponding structure in English.

Akiko-san **wa** me **ga** kiree desu.
Akiko   eyes   pretty are
  | |
topic   subject

Akiko has pretty eyes. [Word-for-word in Japanese: As for Akiko, her eyes are pretty.]

> Topic: *Akiko* because the sentence is about her.
> Subject: *Eyes* because it answers the question "What is pretty?"

Refer to your Japanese textbook for more information.

▼▼▼▼▼▼▼▼▼▼▼▼▼▼▼▼▼REVIEW▼▼▼▼▼▼▼▼▼▼▼▼▼▼▼▼▼

Circle the topic of each sentence in the following sentences.
- Underline the subject of each sentence. (The topic and the subject could be the same word.)

1. Speaking of yesterday, who missed the class? Chris did.

2. Algebra, I can handle.

3. Last year, the Suzukis went to Australia for a vacation.

4. Japan has to import almost all the oil consumed.

23. WHAT IS A PREDICATE?

A sentence can always be divided into two parts: the subject and the predicate (the way to identify subjects is discussed in detail in **What is a Subject?**, p. 70). To put it simply, a predicate is everything in a sentence except the subject; it defines or describes the subject.

A **predicate** can be just one word, a verb for instance, or a group of words containing it. The core of the entire predicate is called the **main predicate** (textbooks often use the terms "predicate" when referring to the "main predicate"). In the examples to follow, the predicate is in *italics* and the main predicate in ***bold italics***.

Mary ***walked***.
　　|　　　　|
subject predicate → main predicate

　　　　　　　　predicate
　　　┌──────────────────────────┐
Mary ***walked*** *to school yesterday morning*.
　　|　　　　|
subject　main predicate

Although in many languages (including English) verbs are the only class of words that can be a main predicate, in other languages (including Japanese) other classes of words can also play that role. In the grammar of such languages, the term "predicate" is a convenient cover term that encompasses all the classes of words that "behave like verbs."

To establish the predicate of a sentence, first find the subject by asking *who* or *what* before the verb. Note that a subject can be more than one word; i.e., a noun and its modifier. Once you have identified the subject, you will know that the rest of the sentence is the predicate.

Those people ***play*** *tennis two hours every day in the park*.
└─────┘ └──────────────────────────────────────┘
　subject　　　　　　　　predicate

Subject: Who plays tennis? → those people
　　　　(*People* is a noun and *those* is its modifier.)
Predicate: play tennis two hours every day in the park
Main predicate: play

Sometimes there are two or more subjects and two or more predicates in a sentence. In order to identify them you have to group words together by meaning. Each unit of a subject + predicate is called a **clause** (see **What are Sentences and Clauses?**, p. 89).

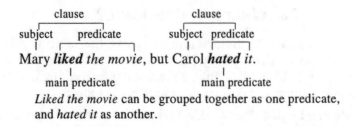

clause   clause

subject   predicate   subject predicate

Mary **liked** *the movie*, but Carol **hated** *it*.

main predicate   main predicate

Liked the movie can be grouped together as one predicate,
and *hated it* as another.

A word such as *but,* as in the above example, is a conjunction and is
not part of the subject or the predicate of the sentence (see **What is a
Conjunction?**, p. 49).

In both English and Japanese it is important to know which predicate
goes with which subject to understand the sentence correctly, especially as sentences become more complex.

IN ENGLISH
A predicate consists of the verb plus all the words in the sentence that
go with it in meaning. The main predicate of a sentence is always a
verb.

Here are examples of predicates whose main predicates are an action
verb, a linking verb *to be* with an adjective, and a linking verb *to be*
with a noun.

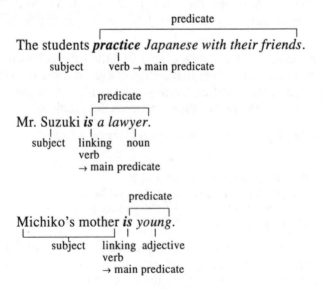

predicate

The students **practice** *Japanese with their friends*.

subject   verb → main predicate

predicate

Mr. Suzuki **is** *a lawyer*.

subject linking noun
verb
→ main predicate

predicate

Michiko's mother **is** *young*.

subject   linking adjective
verb
→ main predicate

IN JAPANESE

The main predicate (often referred to simply as "the predicate") of a sentence can be a verb, the copula **desu** *(to be)*, or an **i**-type adjective. The predicate consists of the main predicate plus all the words in the sentence that go with it in meaning. (See **What is a Descriptive Adjective?**, p. 36, and **What are the Uses of the Verb "To be"?**, p. 26.)

Here are examples of predicates whose main predicates, shown in **bold**, are a verb, the copula **desu** *(to be)*, and an **i**-type adjective.

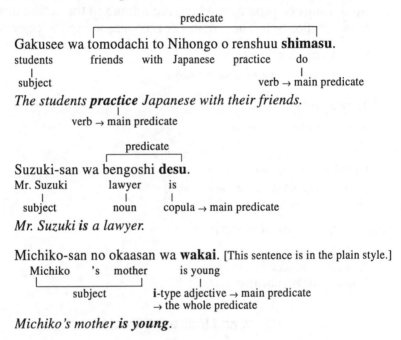

predicate

Gakusee wa tomodachi to Nihongo o renshuu **shimasu**.
students   friends   with   Japanese   practice   do
     subject   verb → main predicate

*The students **practice** Japanese with their friends.*
               verb → main predicate

predicate

Suzuki-san wa bengoshi **desu**.
Mr. Suzuki   lawyer   is
   subject   noun   copula → main predicate

*Mr. Suzuki **is** a lawyer.*

Michiko-san no okaasan wa **wakai**. [This sentence is in the plain style.]
   Michiko   's   mother   is young
            subject   i-type adjective → main predicate
                                → the whole predicate

*Michiko's mother **is young**.*

▼▼▼▼▼▼▼▼▼▼▼▼▼▼▼REVIEW▼▼▼▼▼▼▼▼▼▼▼▼▼▼▼

Underline the entire predicate in the following sentences.
▪ Circle the main predicate.

1. Summer is my favorite season.

2. Nice houses on the beach are quite expensive.

3. The artists' group sponsored a wonderful exhibit with the central theme of world peace.

24. WHAT ARE OBJECTS?

A sentence usually consists, at the very least, of a subject and a main predicate, such as a verb (see **What is a Subject?**, p. 70, and **What is a Predicate?**, p. 79).

> Children play.
> | |
> subject verb

The subject of a sentence is a noun or a pronoun. Many sentences contain other nouns or pronouns which are related to the action of the verb or to a preposition. These nouns or pronouns are called **objects**.

> Ellen writes a *column*.
> | | |
> subject verb   object (common noun)

> They love *her*.
> | | |
> subject | object (pronoun)
>   verb

> I went out with *Paul*.
> | | | |
> | verb preposition object (proper noun)
> subject

There are three types of objects:

  1. direct object
  2. indirect object
  3. object of preposition

Direct and Indirect Objects

IN ENGLISH

Let us see how direct and indirect objects are identified in English.

A **direct object** is a noun or pronoun that receives the action of the verb directly, without a preposition. It answers the question *what?* or *whom?* asked after the verb.[1]

---

[1] In this section, we will consider active sentences only. See **What is Meant by Active and Passive Voice?**, p. 153.

Paul collects *coins.*

> Paul collects what? Coins.
> *Coins* is the direct object.

They see *Paul and Mary.*

> They see whom? Paul and Mary.
> *Paul and Mary* as a group is the direct object.

Do not assume that any word which comes right after a verb is automatically the direct object. It must answer the question *what?* or *whom?*

Paul sees well.

> Paul sees what? No answer.
> Paul sees whom? No answer.

There is no direct object in the sentence. *Well* is an adverb; it answers the question: Paul sees *how?* (see **What is an Adverb?**, p. 40).

An **indirect object** is a noun or pronoun which receives the action of the verb indirectly, with the preposition *to* relating it to the verb. It answers the question *to what?* or *to whom?* asked after the verb.

She spoke *to her friends.*

> She spoke to whom? Her friends.
> *Her friends* is the indirect object.

He gave the painting *to the museum.*

> He gave the painting to what? The museum.
> *The museum* is the indirect object.

IN JAPANESE

In Japanese the direct object is followed by the particle **o** and the indirect object by the particle **ni**.[1] The indirect object typically refers to a person, while the direct object typically refers to a thing.

Direct object → noun or pronoun followed by **o**

Kazuo-san wa **terebi o** mimasu.
Kazuo   television   watches

*Kazuo watches **television**.*

---

[1] In casual conversation, however, the particle **o** is often omitted.

Watashi wa **shinbun to zasshi o** yomimashita.
I   newspaper and magazine   read

*I read the **newspaper and magazine**.*

Notice that when there is more than one object (ex. *newspaper and magazine* in the sentence above), it is sufficient to add just one particle **o** after the last object.

Indirect object→ noun or pronoun followed by **ni**

Okaasan wa **akachan ni** hanashimasu.
mother   baby   to   speaks

*The mother speaks **to her baby**.*

The particle **ni** can indicate other functions besides the indirect object, such as time, place, and purpose. Do not assume that a noun or pronoun followed by **ni** will always be an indirect object (see p. 45).

Sentences with both a Direct and an Indirect Object

IN ENGLISH

A sentence may contain both a direct object and an indirect object. In such a case, the following two word orders are possible:

1. subject (S) + verb (V) + indirect object (IO) + direct object (DO)

Paul gave his sister a gift.
  | | | |
  S   V   IO   DO

Who gave a gift? Paul.→ *Paul* is the subject.
Paul gave what? A gift.→ *A gift* is the direct object.
Paul gave a gift to whom? His sister.
→ *His sister* is the indirect object, even though the preposition "to" does not appear.

2. subject (S) + verb (V) + direct object (DO) + *to* + indirect object (IO)

Paul gave a gift to his sister.
  | | | |
  S   V   DO   IO

Although the word order changes (the direct object precedes the indirect object), the function of each word does not. Be sure to ask the questions to establish the functions of the words in a sentence.

IN JAPANESE
When a sentence contains both a direct and an indirect object, the indirect object + **ni** usually precedes the direct object + **o**. When the speaker wants to emphasize the direct object, the opposite order is possible.

USUALLY—subject **wa** (or **ga**) + indirect object **ni** + direct object **o** + verb

Yoshiko-san wa **watashi ni jisho o** kuremashita.

Yoshiko	me	to	dictionary	gave
|	|___|		|	|
S	IO		DO	V

*Yoshiko gave **me a dictionary**.*
*Yoshiko gave **a dictionary to me**.*

OCCASIONALLY—subject **wa** (or **ga**) + direct object **o** + indirect object **ni** + verb

Yoshiko-san wa **jisho o watashi ni** kuremashita.

Yoshiko	dictionary	me	to	gave
|	|	|___|		|
S	DO	IO		V

*Yoshiko gave **me a dictionary**.*
*Yoshiko gave **a dictionary to me**.*

Object of a Preposition

IN ENGLISH
An object of a preposition is a noun or pronoun which is related to a preposition other than the preposition *to* which marks the indirect object discussed above. An object of a preposition answers the question *what?* or *whom?* asked after the preposition.

Mr. Ito went *with the president*.

Mr. Ito went with whom? With the president.
→ *The president* is the object of the preposition *with*.

IN JAPANESE
The noun or pronoun which precedes a particle is not regarded as an object of the particle in Japanese since the English structure of preposition + noun (or pronoun) object does not exist. Instead, particles are considered to be attached to a noun or pronoun that precedes them.

Honda-san ga **shachoo to** ikimashita.
Mr. Honda   president with   went

*Mr. Honda went **with the president**.*

Careful

The relationship between verb and object is often different in English and Japanese. For example, a verb may take a preposition + an object of the preposition in English but a direct object in Japanese, or a direct object in English but an indirect object in Japanese. Here are some examples of the kinds of differences that you are most likely to encounter.

- object of a preposition in English → direct object in Japanese

  I am looking for the book.
      verb   preposition noun, object of preposition
  Looking for what? The book.
  Function of *the book* is the object of the preposition *for*.

  Hon o sagashite imasu.
   DO particle verb

  Function of **hon** *(book)* is the direct object of the verb **sagashite imasu** *(am looking for)*. Therefore, the particle **o** is used after the noun.

Here is a list of a few common verbs that require an object of a preposition in English, but a direct object in Japanese. The particle **o** is used, therefore, after the noun or pronoun object (represented by the letter "x" below).

to look for "x"	"x" **o** sagashimasu
to look at "x"	"x" **o** mimasu
to wait for "x"	"x" **o** machimasu

- direct object in English → indirect object in Japanese

  *My daughter phones **her friends** every day.*

  Phones whom ? Her friends.
  The function of *her friends* is the direct object of the verb *to phone*.

  Musume wa mainichi **tomodachi ni** denwa o kakemasu.
  daughter   every day friends   to phone call make

  The function of **tomodachi** *(friend)* is the indirect object of the verb **kakemasu** *(to phone)*. Therefore, the particle **ni** is used after the noun.

- direct object in English → not an object in Japanese, but a target or goal followed by the particle **ni**

  Here is a list of a few common verbs that require a direct object in English, but in Japanese use the particle **ni** to mark the target or a goal (represented by the letter "x" below) of the action of the verb.

to meet "x"	"x" **ni** aimasu
to touch "x"	"x" **ni** sawarimasu
to become "x"	"x" **ni** narimasu
to resemble "x"	"x" **ni** nimasu

When you learn a Japanese verb it is important that you learn the type of object it takes so that you will know which particle to use with the noun.

Summary

There are three types of objects in a sentence; a direct object, an indirect object, and an object of preposition.

DIRECT OBJECT—An object which receives the action of the verb directly, without a preposition, is called a direct object. It is followed by the particle **o** in Japanese.

INDIRECT OBJECT—An object which receives the action of the verb indirectly, through the preposition *to*, is called an indirect object. It is followed by the particle **ni** in Japanese. If a direct object is also present in the sentence, the indirect object will typically refer to a person, and the direct object will typically refer to a thing.

OBJECT OF A PREPOSITION—An object which is related to a preposition (other than the preposition *to* which marks an indirect object) is called an object of a preposition. A noun or pronoun followed by a particle is not regarded as an object of the particle in Japanese.

Always identify the function of a word within the language in which you are working; do not mix English and Japanese patterns.

▼▼▼▼▼▼▼▼▼▼▼▼▼▼▼▼▼▼REVIEW▼▼▼▼▼▼▼▼▼▼▼▼▼▼▼▼▼▼

Find the objects in the following sentences:
- Next to Q, write the question you need to ask to find the object.
- Next to A, write the answer to the question you just asked.
- In the column to the right, identify the kind of object it is by circling the appropriate letters: Direct object (DO), Indirect object (IO), or Object of a preposition (OP).

1. The children brought a kitten home.

Q: _____

A: _____   DO   IO   OP

2. The Red Cross sends food and medical equipment to people in need.

Q: _____

A: _____   DO   IO   OP

Q: _____

A: _____   DO   IO   OP

3. The parents paid for the books with a credit card.

Q: _____

A: _____   DO   IO   OP

Q: _____

A: _____   DO   IO   OP

25. WHAT ARE SENTENCES AND CLAUSES?

What is a Sentence?

A **sentence** is the expression of a complete thought. Typically a sentence consists of at least a subject and a main predicate, such as a verb (see **What is a Subject?**, p. 70, **What is a Predicate?**, p. 79, and **What is a Verb?**, p. 21). In writing, the end of a sentence is marked by a period, a question mark or an exclamation mark.

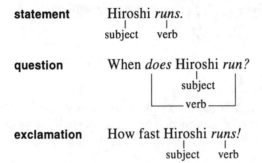

statement   Hiroshi *runs.*
                   subject   verb

question   When *does* Hiroshi *run?*
                                subject
                                verb

exclamation   How fast Hiroshi *runs!*
                            subject   verb

Depending on the verb, a sentence may also have direct and indirect objects (see **What are Objects?**, p. 82).

We saw a *movie.*
subject   direct object
     verb

Kazuko gave *Hiroshi* a present.
subject verb indirect   direct
               object   object

In addition, a sentence may include various kinds of modifiers, such as adjectives, adverbs, and prepositional phrases (see **What is an Adjective?**, p. 35, **What is an Adverb?**, p. 40, and **What is a Preposition?**, p. 44).

We saw a *great* movie.
adjective modifying *movie*

We saw a great movie *yesterday.*
adverb modifying *saw*

We saw a great movie *after work.*
prepositional phrase modifying *saw*

IN ENGLISH
There is no set position for the verb in an English sentence, but the subject almost always comes before the verb.

We *went* to a concert.
subject verb

Certain types of modifiers can also come before the subject.

Yesterday we went to a concert.
adverb modifying *went*

IN JAPANESE
The main predicate (i.e., a verb, the copula, or an **i**-type adjective) always appears at the end of a sentence. The subject usually appears at the beginning of a sentence, but is omitted if it is understood by the context.

Watashi wa kinoo tomodachi ni tegami o **kakimashita.**
I yesterday friend to letter wrote
subject adverb indirect object direct object verb

*I **wrote** a letter to my friend yesterday.*

Senkoo wa keezai **desu.**
major economics is
subject copula

*My major **is** economics.*

Nihongo wa totemo **omoshiroi desu.**
Japanese very is interesting
subject adverb **i**-type adj polite marker

*Japanese **is** very **interesting**.*

Certain types of modifiers can also come before the subject.

Kinoo watashi wa tomodachi ni tegami o kakimashita.
yesterday I friend to letter wrote
adverb subject indirect object direct object verb

***Yesterday** I wrote a letter to my friend.*

In Japanese a period is usually used in place of a question mark and exclamation mark, as long as the particles **ka** (for questions) and **ne** (for tag questions and exclamations) appear at the end of a sentence (see **What are Declarative and Interrogative Sentences?**, p. 97).

Hiroshi-san wa itsu hashirimasu **ka**.
Hiroshi   when   run
  | | |
subject   adverb   verb
When does Hiroshi run?

Hiroshi-san wa hayaku hashiremasu **ne**.
Hiroshi   fast   can run
  | | |
subject   adverb   verb
How fast Hiroshi can run!

What is a Clause?

A clause is a group of words that contains its own subject and predicate, such as a verb. Simply put, a clause is a sentence within a sentence or within another clause.

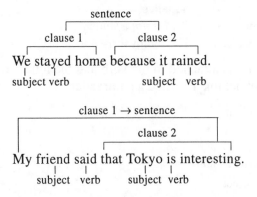

You will find more details on various types of sentences and clauses in **What are the Different Types of Sentences and Clauses?**, p. 167.

26. WHAT ARE AFFIRMATIVE AND NEGATIVE SENTENCES?

A sentence can be classified as to whether it states a fact or situation that is, or a fact or situation that is not. An **affirmative sentence** states a fact or situation that is; it *affirms* the information.

> Japan is a country in Asia.
> Mr. Inoue will work at the bank.
> They liked to travel.

A **negative sentence** states a fact or situation that is not; it *negates* the information. It includes an element of negation.

> Japan is *not* a country in Europe.
> Mr. Inoue will *not* work at the library.
> They did *not* like to stay home.

IN ENGLISH

An affirmative sentence can become a negative sentence in one of three ways:

1. by adding the word **not** after a form of the verb *to be* (see **What are the Uses of the Verb "To be"?**, p. 26)

Affirmative	→	Negative
Tom is a student.		Tom *is not* a student.
The rooms were clean.		The rooms *were not* clean.

Frequently, the word *not* is attached to the verb and the letter "o" is replaced by an apostrophe; this is called a **contraction**.

> Tom *isn't* a student.
> |
>   is not

> The rooms *weren't* clean.
> |
>   were not

2. by adding the word **not** after auxiliary verbs, such as *can, should,* and *will* (see **What is an Auxiliary Verb?**, p. 31)

Mary *can* do it.	Mary *cannot* do it.
You *should* drive.	You *should not* drive.
They *will* eat sushi.	They *will not* eat sushi.

Frequently, *can, should*, etc. are contracted with *not*: *can't, shouldn't*, etc. The contracted form of *will not* is *won't*.

Mary *can't* do it.
|
cannot

They *won't* eat sushi.
|
will not

3. by adding the auxiliary verb *do, does,* or *did + not* to the dictionary form of the main verb. *Do* or *does* is used for negatives in the present tense and *did* for negatives in the past tense (see **What is the Present Tense?**, p. 136, and **What is the Past Tense?**, p. 142).

Affirmative	→	**Negative**
We study a lot.		We *do not* study a lot.
Mary writes well.		Mary *does not* write well.
The train arrived.		The train *did not* arrive.

Frequently, *do, does,* or *did* is contracted with *not: don't, doesn't, didn't.*

The regular word order in English negative sentences is: tense word *(do, does, did,* or *will)* + negative word *(not* or *n't)* + verb.

We *do not study* a lot.
  └─┬─┘ │
     verb
 present negative

The train *did not arrive.*
    └─┬─┘ │
       verb
   past negative

IN JAPANESE

An affirmative sentence can become a negative sentence by changing the main predicate (a verb, the copula *to be,* or an **i**-type adjective) to its negative form.

While the tense and negative elements such as *did* and *not* in English are independent words, in Japanese they are suffixes that are attached to the end of a main predicate (see **What are Prefixes and Suffixes?**, p. 53). Unlike English where the tense and the negative words precede the verb, in Japanese the order of appearance is the following: verb + negative suffix + tense suffix.

Densha wa **ki*masen*deshita**.
train   arrive-not- past
        | | |
      verb neg. tense

*The train **did not arrive**.*
        | | |
     tense neg. verb

Here are some examples of affirmative and negative forms of the various main predicates (verbs, the copula and the **i**-type adjectives) in the nonpast and past tenses in the polite style. (See your textbook for other forms.)

VERBS

NONPAST   **affirmative:**   **-masu**
                negative: **-masen**

Nonpast affirmative	→	**Nonpast negative**
yomi**masu**		yomi**masen**
read, will read		*do (does) not read,* **will not** *read*

    Tanaka-san wa shinbun o **yomi*masu***.
    *Mr. Tanaka **reads** the paper.*

    Tanaka-san wa shinbun o **yomi*masen***.
    *Mr. Tanaka **doesn't read** the paper.*

PAST   **affirmative:**   **-mashita**
           negative: **-masendeshita**
                     (nonpast negative form (**-masen**) + **-deshita**)

Past affirmative	→	**Past negative**
yomi**mashita**		yomi**masendeshita**
read		*did not read*

    Tanaka-san wa shinbun o **yomi*mashita***.
    *Mr. Tanaka **read** the paper.*

    Tanaka-san wa shinbun o **yomi*masendeshita***.
    *Mr. Tanaka **didn't read** the paper.*

COPULA—A form of the copula *(to be)* is attached to nouns and **na**-type adjective stems (see **What are the Uses of the Verb "To be"?**, p. 26).

NONPAST   **affirmative:**   **desu**
                negative: **dewa arimasen**

Nonpast affirmative	→	**Nonpast negative**
gakusee **desu**		gakusee **dewa arimasen**
is a student		*is **not** a student*

Chin-san wa gakusee **desu.**
Ms. Chin is a student.

Chin-san wa gakusee **dewa arimasen.**
Ms. Chin isn't a student.

PAST   **affirmative: deshita**
        negative: dewa arimasendeshita
                (nonpast negative form (**dewa arimasen**) + **deshita**)

Past affirmative   →   **Past negative**
gakusee **deshita**   gakusee **dewa arimasendeshita**
was a student   *was not a student*

Chin-san wa gakusee **deshita.**
Ms. Chin was a student.

Chin-san wa gakusee **dewa arimasendeshita.**
Ms. Chin wasn't a student.

Frequently, the particle combination **dewa** in **dewa arimasen** and **dewa arimasendeshita** is contracted to **ja.**

Chin-san wa gakusee **ja arimasen.**
                            |
                          dewa
Ms. Chin isn't a student.

Chin-san wa gakusee **ja arimasendeshita.**
                            |
                          dewa
Ms. Chin wasn't a student.

I-TYPE ADJECTIVES

NONPAST   **affirmative: -i desu**
           negative: -ku arimasen
           or   **-ku nai desu**

Nonpast affirmative   →   **Nonpast negative**
taka**i desu**   taka**ku arimasen**
is expensive   taka**ku nai desu**
                                is not expensive

Kono kuruma wa **taka***i desu.*
This car is expensive.

Kono kuruma wa **taka***ku arimasen.*
Kono kuruma wa **taka***ku nai desu.*
This car isn't expensive.

PAST	affirmative:	**-katta desu**
	negative:	**-ku arimasendeshita**
		(nonpast negative form (**-ku arimasen**) + **-deshita**)
	or	**-ku nakatta desu**
		(nonpast negative stem (**-ku na-**) + **-katta desu**)

Past affirmative	→	**Past negative**
taka**katta desu**		taka**ku arimasendeshita**
was expensive		taka**ku nakatta desu**
		*was **not** expensive*

Kono kuruma wa taka***katta desu***.
*This car **was expensive**.*

Kono kuruma wa taka***ku arimasendeshita***.
Kono kuruma wa taka***ku nakatta desu***.
*This car **wasn't expensive**.*

Careful
Remember that there is no equivalent for the auxiliary verbs *do*, *does*, *did*, or *will* in Japanese; do not try to include them.

▼▼▼▼▼▼▼▼▼▼▼▼▼▼▼▼▼REVIEW▼▼▼▼▼▼▼▼▼▼▼▼▼▼▼▼▼▼

Write the negative of the affirmative sentences below.

1. Masashi speaks French.

_____

2. I exercise every day.

_____

3. Japanese grammar is difficult.

_____

4. The winds were strong last night.

_____

5. We will go sailing tomorrow.

_____

27. WHAT ARE DECLARATIVE AND INTERROGATIVE SENTENCES?

A sentence can be classified according to its purpose.

A **declarative sentence** is a sentence that is a statement; it states the information.

> Commodore Perry came to Japan in 1853.

An **interrogative sentence** is a sentence that asks a question.

> When did Commodore Perry come to Japan?

Types of Interrogative Sentences

Interrogative sentences, i.e., questions, can be classified into three types: yes-or-no questions, "wh"-questions and tag questions.

A *yes*-or-*no* **question** is used when you expect an answer with "yes" or "no."

> **question** Did you go to the library last night?
> **answer** Yes, I did. *or* No, I didn't.

A *wh*-**question** (also called an **information question**) contains **interrogative words** (or wh-**words**), such as *who, what, when, where, why*, and *how* (see **What is an Interrogative Word?**, p. 102). These questions, which cannot be answered with "yes" or "no," are used when you want to obtain information.

> **question** Where did you go last night?
> **answer** I went to the library.

A **tag question** is used when you want to confirm your belief. As with a yes-or-no question, you expect an answer with "yes" or "no."

> **question** You went to the library last night, didn't you?
> **answer** Yes, I did. *or* No, I didn't.

While all written questions end with a question mark in English, in Japanese they usually end with a period. Let us look at the various types of questions and see how each type is handled.

Yes-or-No Questions

IN ENGLISH

A declarative sentence can be changed to a yes-or-no question in one of two ways:

1. by using an **inversion** of the subject and the verb *to be* or of the subject and an auxiliary verb. In other words, the normal word order of subject + verb is changed to verb + subject (see **What are the Uses of the Verb "To be"?**, p. 26, and **What is an Auxiliary Verb?**, p. 31).

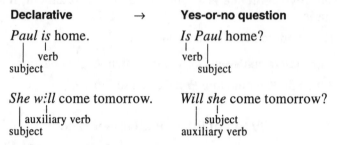

Declarative	→	Yes-or-no question

Paul is home. ⎵ verb ⎵ subject

Is Paul home? verb ⎵ subject

She will come tomorrow. ⎵ auxiliary verb ⎵ subject

Will she come tomorrow? ⎵ subject ⎵ auxiliary verb

2. by adding the auxiliary verb *do, does,* or *did* before the subject and changing the main verb to the dictionary form of the verb. *Do* and *does* are used to introduce a question in the present tense and *did* to introduce a question in the past tense (see **What is the Present Tense?**, p. 136, and **What is the Past Tense?**, p. 142).

Declarative	→	Yes-or-no question
Tom *likes* baseball.		*Does* Tom *like* baseball?
They *sing* together.		*Do* they *sing* together?
Ann *went* to Nara.		*Did* Ann *go* to Nara?

IN JAPANESE

A declarative sentence can be changed to a *yes-or-no* question by adding the particle **ka** at the end of a sentence, usually without a question mark. Inversion is never used in Japanese to form a question.

declarative	Suzuki-san wa yakyuu o yarimasu.
	Mr. Suzuki plays baseball.
interrogative	Suzuki-san wa yakyuu o yarimasu **ka**.
	Does Mr. Suzuki play baseball?
declarative	Arisu-san wa Amerika-jin desu.
	Alice is an American.
interrogative	Arisu-san wa Amerika-jin desu **ka**.
	Is Alice an American?

Make sure that you ignore *do, does*, and *did* when you are using Japanese. They signal a question in English, but they are not translated.

"*Wh-*" Questions

IN ENGLISH

A declarative sentence can be turned into a "wh-"question by first changing it to a *yes*-or-*no* question and then placing the appropriate interrogative word for the information you want to obtain at the beginning of the question.

Declarative	→	Yes-or-no question	→	"wh"-question
Tom likes baseball.		Does Tom like *baseball?*		*What* does Tom like?
Ann went to Nara.		Did Ann go *to Nara?*		*Where* did Ann go?

IN JAPANESE

A declarative sentence can be changed to a "wh"-question by using an interrogative word for the information you want to obtain and adding the particle **ka** at the end of the sentence. Unlike in English where an interrogative word, regardless of its function, is always placed at the beginning of the interrogative sentence, in Japanese the interrogative word occupies the same place in the interrogative sentence that it occupies in the declarative sentence, namely, the position dictated by its function. Since the function of the interrogative word remains the same, the particle attached to it remains the same. The only exception is that an interrogative word as subject must be marked with the particle **ga**, and never **wa**.

declarative	Suzuki-san wa **yakyuu o** yarimasu.
	yakyuu *(baseball)* → direct object
	Mr. Suzuki plays baseball.
wh-question	Suzuki-san wa **nani o** yarimasu **ka.**
	nani *(what)* → direct object
	What does Mr. Suzuki play?

declarative	Suzuki-san ga yakyuu o yarimasu.
	Suzuki-san *(Mr. Suzuki)* → subject
	Mr. Suzuki plays baseball.
wh-question	**Dare ga** yakyuu o yarimasu **ka.**
	date *(who)* → subject
	Who plays baseball?

Tag Questions

IN ENGLISH

A declarative sentence can be changed to a question by adding a short phrase, sometimes called a **tag**, at the end of the statement. If a sentence is affirmative, the tag repeats the idea of the statement as a negative question. If a sentence is negative, the tag repeats the idea of the statement as an affirmative question. A comma is always inserted between the original statement and the tag.

Mr. Suzuki *plays* baseball, *doesn't he*?
  affirmative   negative

Tom and Ann *are* Americans, *aren't they*?
  affirmative   negative

This *isn't* a Japanese stamp, *is it*?
negative   affirmative

Emiko *didn't go* to Nara, *did she*?
  negative   affirmative

IN JAPANESE

The particle **ne** can be added at the end of a declarative sentence to turn it into something similar in meaning to a tag question. The original sentence can be either affirmative or negative. Neither a question mark nor a comma is used in Japanese tag questions.

Suzuki-san wa yakyuu o yarimasu **ne**.
*Mr. Suzuki plays baseball, **doesn't he**?*

Tomu-san to An-san wa Amerika-jin desu **ne**.
*Tom and Ann are Americans, **aren't they**?*

Kore wa Nihon no kitte ja arimasen **ne**.
*This isn't a Japanese stamp, **is it**?*

Emiko-san wa Nara e ikimasendeshita **ne**.
*Emiko didn't go to Nara, **did she**?*

Notice that although the particle **ne** never changes, the English equivalent does.

▼▼▼▼▼▼▼▼▼▼▼▼▼▼▼▼REVIEW▼▼▼▼▼▼▼▼▼▼▼▼▼▼▼▼

I. Write the yes-or-no question which corresponds to the declarative sentences below.

1. Hajime and Yoshiko studied all evening.

_____

2. Mr. Honda works for an automobile company.

_____

3. California will be dry this summer.

_____

II. Change the declarative sentences below into a *wh*-question asking for the italicized information.

1. Akiko is studying *psychology* in college.

_____

2. They lived in Arizona *last year*.

_____

3. *Mr. Ito* likes to sing karaoke.

_____

III. Change the declarative sentences below into tag questions.

1. They are planning to raise taxes.

_____

2. It doesn't snow around here.

_____

3. The new movie is very funny.

_____

28. WHAT IS AN INTERROGATIVE WORD?

An **interrogative word** is a word that asks a question. The term *interrogative* comes from *interrogate,* to question. According to their part of speech, these words can be classified into three categories: interrogative pronouns, interrogative adjectives, and interrogative adverbs.

Interrogative Pronoun

An **interrogative pronoun** is a word that replaces a noun and introduces a question (see **What is a Pronoun?**, p. 7).

IN ENGLISH
Different interrogative pronouns are used depending on whether you are referring to people or "things" (this category includes objects and ideas, and sometimes animals).

PEOPLE —The interrogative pronoun referring to people changes according to its grammatical function in the sentence; *who* is used for the subject, *whom* is used for the direct object, indirect object, and the object of a preposition, and *whose* is used to ask about possession or ownership.

> *Who* lives here?
> |
> subject

> *Whom* do you know?
> |
> direct object

> From *whom* did you receive the roses?
> |
> object of preposition *from*

> *Whose* pen is this?
> |
> possessive

In informal English, *who* is often used instead of *whom,* and prepositions are placed at the end of the sentence, separated from the interrogative pronoun to which they are linked.

> *Who* do you know?
> |
> instead of *whom*

Who did you receive the roses *from*?
| |
instead of *whom*   preposition

THINGS —The interrogative pronoun *what* refers only to things, and the same form is used for subject, direct object, indirect object, and the object of a preposition.

What happened?
|
subject

What will you buy?
|
direct object

What do you cook it with?
|
object of preposition *with*

IN JAPANESE

As in English a different interrogative pronoun is used depending on whether the pronoun replaces a person or a thing. Unlike English, however, interrogative pronouns themselves do not change according to their functions; instead, the particles that are attached to them change. Note that interrogative adverbs such as *when* and *where* in English (see p. 107) are interrogative pronouns in Japanese.

Interrogative pronoun replacing:

person	**dare**	*who*
thing	**nani**	*what*
place	**doko**	*where, which place*
time	**itsu**	*when*

Let us look at these interrogative pronouns in sentences. Notice that the appropriate particle follows the interrogative pronoun to indicate its function.

Dare ga kimasu ka.
|
subject particle
Who is coming?

Dare ni agemasu ka.
|
indirect object particle
Who will you give it to?

Kore wa **dare no** pen desu ka.
                 possessive particle
Whose pen is this?

Nani o kaimasu ka.
direct object particle
What will you buy?

Doko o sooji shimashoo ka.
direct object particle
Where shall I clean?

Itsu ga ii desu ka.
subject particle
When will be the best time?

"Which One," "Which Ones"

There is another interrogative pronoun which we will now examine separately because it does not follow the same pattern as those above.

IN ENGLISH
Which one, *which ones* can refer to both persons and things; they are used in questions that request the selection of one (*which one*, singular) or several (*which ones*, plural) from a group. The words *one* and *ones* are often omitted. These interrogative pronouns may be used as a subject, direct object, indirect object, and object of a preposition.

All the teachers are here. *Which one* teaches English?
                              singular subject

There are many guests. *Which ones* came from Japan?
                           plural subject

I have two umbrellas. *Which one* do you want to take?
                         singular direct object

IN JAPANESE
There are two basic interrogative pronouns which imply selection, **dochira** and **dore**. You will use one or the other depending on the overall number from which the selection is made; i.e., selection from two or from three or more.

- which one of the two persons or things → **dochira**
- which one of the three or more things → **dore**
- which one of the three or more persons → **dono hito**
  (which person) interrogative adjective (**dono**) + noun (**hito**)

The particle that is attached to the interrogative pronoun indicates its function in a sentence.

Onna no hito ga futari imasu ne. **Dochira ga** Itoo-san desu ka.
female persons   two   there are   which one | Ms. Ito   is
                                              |
                                    subject particle

*There are two women. **Which one** is Ms. Ito?*

Dochira no nekutai ga ii desu ka.
  which 's   tie   is good
  |
  possessive particle

***Which tie** (of the two) is better?*

Kasa ga takusan arimasu ga, **dore o** kaimashoo ka.
umbrella many   there are but which | shall we buy
                               one |
                            direct object particle

*There are many umbrellas; **which one** shall we buy?*

Dono hito ni kikeba ii desu ka.
which person to   ask if is good
                |
      indirect object particle

***Which person** should I ask?*

Interrogative Adjective

An **interrogative adjective** is a word that modifies a noun and introduces a question (see **What is an Adjective?**, p. 35).

IN ENGLISH

Which and *what* are called interrogative adjectives when they come in front of a noun and are used to ask a question about that noun. (An interrogative pronoun, on the other hand, replaces a noun.)

Which teacher is teaching the course?
  | |
interr. adj. noun

What courses are you taking?
| |
interr. adj. noun

What are you taking?
|
interr. pronoun (replaces a noun; no noun follows it)

IN JAPANESE

There are three interrogative adjectives:

- **dono** → *which*
- **donna** → *what type of*
- **doo yuu** → *what type of*

Donna and **doo yuu** are almost interchangeable, but **donna** sounds more informal than **doo yuu**.

Just as in English, interrogative adjectives in Japanese come in front of the noun they modify and are used to ask a question about that noun.

Dono sensee ga sono koosu o oshiete imasu ka.
which teacher   that course   teaching   is
| |
interr. adj.   noun
Which teacher is teaching that course?

Donna (*or* **Doo yuu**) eega ga suki desu ka.
what type of   movies   like
| |
interrogative adjective   noun
What type of movies do you like?

Careful

The word *what* is not always an interrogative adjective. If it replaces a noun it is an interrogative pronoun; if it modifies a noun, it is an interrogative adjective. It is important that you distinguish one from the other because different words are used in Japanese.

What courses are you taking?
| |
interr. adj. noun

Dono koosu o totte imasu ka.
| |
interr. adj. noun

What are you taking?
|
interr. pronoun

Nani o totte imasu ka.
|
interr. pronoun

Interrogative Adverb

An **interrogative adverb** is a word that modifies a verb, an adjective, or another adverb, and introduces a question (see **What is an Adverb?**, p. 40).

IN ENGLISH
Where, *when*, *how* and *why* are called interrogative adverbs. They are used to ask a question about place, time, manner and reason, respectively.

Where were you born?
|
asks about place

How do you make sushi?
|
asks about manner

IN JAPANESE
Words such as **doo, doo yatte** *(how)* and **naze, doo shite** *(why)* are called interrogative adverbs. Some interrogative pronouns such as **itsu** *(when)*, **ikutsu** *(how many)*, and **ikura** *(how much)* can function as adverbs as well. Interrogative adverbs are not followed by a particle to indicate function.

Osushi wa **doo yatte** tsukuru n desu ka.
sushi   how   make
How do you make sushi?

Okane wa **ikura** motte imasu ka.
money   how much   have
How much money do you have?

Naze and **doo shite** *(why)* are almost interchangeable, but **doo** and **doo yatte** *(how)* are not. Refer to your textbook for more information.

▼▼▼▼▼▼▼▼▼▼▼▼▼▼▼▼▼REVIEW▼▼▼▼▼▼▼▼▼▼▼▼▼▼▼▼▼

I. Circle the interrogative pronoun in the sentences below.
- Indicate whether the interrogative pronoun is a subject (s), direct object (DO), indirect object (IO), or possessive (POSS).

1. What shall we plant here?	S	DO	IO	POSS
2. What is under the carpet?	S	DO	IO	POSS
3. Whose shirt are your wearing?	S	DO	IO	POSS

II. Circle the Japanese equivalent of the expression *which one* in the following sentences: **dochira** (*which thing/person* out of two selections), **dore** (*which thing* out of three or more selections) or **dono hito** (*which person* out of three or more selections).

1. I bought all the books for this course. *Which one* should I read first?

dochira   **dore**   **dono hito**

2. There are only two cookies left. *Which one* do you want?

dochira   **dore**   **dono hito**

3. I see many people there. *Which one* is your brother?

dochira   **dore**   **dono hito**

III. Circle the interrogative adjective in the following sentences.
- Draw an arrow from the interrogative adjective to the noun it modifies.

1. Please tell me what time the game starts.

2. Which hotel are you staying at?

IV. Circle the interrogative adverb in each of the following sentences.

1. When do you expect to be back?

2. Why didn't you leave a message?

3. How do you open this box?

29. WHAT IS A DEMONSTRATIVE WORD?

A **demonstrative word** is a word that is used to point to something or to refer to something which has been mentioned before. The term *demonstrative* comes from *demonstrate,* to show. According to their part of speech, these words can be classified into three categories: demonstrative pronouns, demonstrative adjectives, and demonstrative adverbs.

IN ENGLISH
Demonstrative words indicate the distance between the speaker and the person or thing spoken about.

> *This* radio is cheaper than *that* one.
> close to speaker   far from speaker

IN JAPANESE
All Japanese demonstrative words start with the sound **ko-**, **so-**, or **a-** depending on the distance between the speaker, the listener, and the person or thing referred to.

ko- → the person or thing is near the speaker or near both the speaker and the listener

so- → the person or thing is near the listener only

a- → the person or thing is far from both the speaker and the listener

Let us look at the various demonstrative words according to their part of speech; pronoun, adjective, or adverb.

Demonstrative Pronoun

A **demonstrative pronoun** is a word that is used instead of a noun to point to someone or something, or to refer to someone or something previously mentioned (see **What is a Pronoun?**, p. 7).

IN ENGLISH
The singular demonstrative pronouns are *this (one)* and *that (one)* the plural forms are *these* and *those*. *This (one)* and *these* refer to a person or a thing near the speaker, and *that (one)* and *those* refer to a person or a thing away from the speaker.

Are those your suitcases?—*This* is mine but *that* is not.

pointing to a suitcase   pointing to a suitcase
close to speaker   far from speaker

The books are on the shelves. *These* are in Japanese, *those* in English.

pointing to books   pointing to books
close to speaker   far from speaker

IN JAPANESE

Demonstrative pronouns are used to refer to things or places, and not usually people. When referring to people, the demonstrative adjective is used (see below). Unlike English, Japanese demonstrative pronouns do not distinguish singular and plural forms; for example, *this* and *these* are expressed by the same word. The form of the demonstrative pronoun is determined by the distance between the speaker, the listener, and the thing or place referred to.

- the thing or place is near the speaker (or near both the speaker and the listener)

kore	→	this thing, these things
koko	→	this place, here
kochira	→	this direction, this way

- the thing or place is near the listener only

sore	→	that thing, those things
soko	→	that place, there
sochira	→	that direction, that way

- the thing or place is far from both the speaker and the listener

are	→	that thing, those things (far away)
asoko	→	that place, over there (far away)
achira	→	that direction, that way

Here are some examples. Notice the appropriate particle following the demonstrative pronoun to indicate its function.

- to point to things

  Kore wa watashi no kaban desu ga, **sore wa** chigaimasu.

this   I   's suitcase is but   that   is not

This is my suitcase, but that (near you) is not.

  Are wa nan desu ka.

What is that (far away)?

- to point to places

> **Koko ga** daidokoro de, **asoko ga** shinshitsu desu.
> this   kitchen is and that   bedroom   is
>
> *This is a kitchen, and that over there is a bedroom.*

- to point to directions

> Otearai **wa sochira** desu.
> restroom   that way   is
>
> *The restroom is that way.*

Demonstrative Adjective

A **demonstrative adjective** is a word that modifies a noun and point out a person or a thing (see **What is an Adjective?**, p. 35).

IN ENGLISH

This and *that* in the singular and *these* and *those* in the plural are called demonstrative adjectives when they come in front of a noun. (A demonstrative pronoun, on the other hand, replaces a noun.)

> *This* book is interesting.
> | |
> dem. adj. noun

> *This* is interesting.
> |
> dem. pronoun (no noun follows it)

Just as when *this, that, these,* and *those* function as pronoun, the adjectives *this* and *these* point to a person or thing near the speaker, and *that* and *those* point to a person or thing away from the speaker.

Singular	Plural
this car	*these* cars
that man	*those* men

A demonstrative adjective always precedes the noun it modifies. If there is a descriptive adjective, it is placed between the demonstrative adjective and the noun (see **What is a Descriptive Adjective?**, p. 36).

> I want *this* camera.
> | |
>   dem. adj. noun

That sweater is pretty.

dem. adj. noun

That blue sweater is pretty.

dem.   descrip. noun
adj.   adj.

IN JAPANESE

Demonstrative adjectives are used to point to people and things. Unlike English, Japanese demonstrative adjectives do not distinguish singular and plural forms; for example, *this* and *these* are expressed by the same word. There are three sets of demonstrative adjectives in Japanese:

kono, sono, ano	→	*this, that*
konna, sonna, anna	→	*this type of, that type of*
koo yuu, soo yuu, aa yuu	→	*this type of, that type of*

The words in the last two sets are almost interchangeable, but the last set is the more formal of the two.

- the person or thing is near the speaker (or near both the speaker and the listener)

kono	→	*this, these*
konna or **koo yuu**	→	*this type of, these types of*

- the person or thing is near the listener only

sono	→	*that, those*
sonna or **soo yuu**	→	*that type of, those types of*

- the person or thing is far from both the speaker and the listener

ano	→	*that, those*
anna or **aa yuu**	→	*that type of, those types of*

The demonstrative adjective can be used to point to people, as well as to things. When it is used to refer to people, you must add the word **hito** *(person)* after the demonstrative adjective, even if in English the pronoun *this* or *that* is used alone.

Ano hito wa dare desu ka. [Person is far from the listener and the speaker.]

that   person   who   is

*Who is **that** (person)?*

Just as in English, demonstrative adjectives in Japanese precede the noun they modify and point to that noun.

Kono kamera wa benri desu.
dem. adj. noun

This camera is handy. [The camera is near the speaker.]

Sonna kamera ga hoshii desu.
dem. adj. noun

*I want **that kind of** camera.* [The camera is near the listener.]

As in English, a demonstrative adjective usually precedes the noun it modifies. If there is a descriptive adjective, it is usually placed between the demonstrative adjective and the noun (see **What is a Descriptive Adjective?**, p. 36).

Ano seetaa wa yasui desu.
dem. noun
adj.

That sweater is inexpensive.
dem. noun
adj.

Ano akai seetaa wa yasui desu.
dem. descrip. noun
adj. adj.

That red sweater is inexpensive.

Careful

It is important that you distinguish between *this, these* and *that, those* functioning as adjectives and those functioning as pronouns in English because different words are used in Japanese; **kono, konna, koo yuu** for adjectives and **kore, koko, kochira** for pronouns.

This watch is mine. → **Kono** tokee wa watashi no desu.
dem. noun   dem. noun
adj.   adj.

This is mine. → **Kore** wa watashi no desu.
dem. pronoun   dem. pronoun

Demonstrative Adverb

A **demonstrative adverb** is a word used to point out the manner in which something is done. (See **What is an Adverb?**, p. 40).

IN ENGLISH
We have thus far seen that *this*, *that* and *these*, *those* can function as demonstrative pronouns and adjectives. The same words can also function as demonstrative adverbs. In addition, phrases such as *this way, that way, in this manner, in that manner,* and *like this, like that* function as demonstrative adverbs. Unlike adjectives which can only modify nouns, adverbs modify verbs, adjectives or other adverbs.

This indicates that what is spoken about is close to the speaker, while phrases with *that* indicate that what is spoken about is closer to the listener or a third party.

> I've never tasted anything *this* good.
>   dem.   adjective
>   adverb

> Takeshi is a good runner. I cannot run *that* fast.
>   dem.   adverb
>   adverb

> Please do it *this way*. Okay, I'll do it *that way*.
>   verb   dem. adverb   verb   dem. adverb

IN JAPANESE
Words such as **koo** *(in this manner)*, **soo**, **aa** *(in that manner)* and **konna ni** *(like this)*, **sonna ni**, **anna ni** *(like that)* are called demonstrative adverbs. As in English, they modify verbs, adjectives, and other adverbs. Phrases with the sound **ko** are used when pointing to something close to the speaker, phrases with **so** when pointing to something close to the listener, and phrases with **a** when pointing to something far away from both the speaker and the listener.

Konna ni oishii mono wa tabeta koto ga arimasen.
dem. adverb   adjective
*I've never tasted anything **this** good.*
modifies adjective *good*

Ano hito wa hayai desu ne. Watashi wa **anna ni** hayaku hashiremasen.
dem. adverb   adverb
*That person is fast! I cannot run **that** fast.*
modifies adverb *fast*

Koo shite kudasai. Hai, **soo** shimasu.
this way do please   okay that way will do
dem.   verb   dem.   verb
adverb   adverb
*Please do it **this way**. Okay, I'll do it **that way**.*
modifies verb *do*

Careful

Unlike *this* and *that* in English, which can be used as pronouns, adjectives or adverbs, Japanese demonstrative adverbs (ex. **koo, konna ni**) are not interchangeable with demonstrative pronouns (ex. **kore, koko, kochira**) or demonstrative adjectives (ex. **kono, konna, koo yuu**).

▼▼▼▼▼▼▼▼▼▼▼▼▼▼▼▼▼REVIEW▼▼▼▼▼▼▼▼▼▼▼▼▼▼▼▼▼

I. Circle the appropriate word to complete the following paragraph.

The demonstrative pronoun expressing *this* and *these* in Japanese is
(1) **kore   sore   are** , when referring to a thing close to the speaker
or close to both the speaker and the listener. When a thing is close to
the listener only, (2) **kore   sore   are** is used. When a thing is far from
both the speaker and the listener, (3) **kore   sore   are** is used. **Koko**,
soko, and **asoko** are demonstrative pronouns referring to (4) *people*
places   manners.

II. Circle the demonstrative adjective in the following sentences.
▪ Draw an arrow from the demonstrative adjective to the noun it modifies.

1. They prefer that candidate.

2. This food is delicious.

3. You paid too much for those sneakers.

4. These houses are more expensive than those.

III. Circle the demonstrative adverb in the following sentences.
▪ Draw an arrow from the demonstrative adverb to the word it modifies.

1. The pianist was marvelous. I can't play the piece that well.

2. I've never tried anything this hard.

3. First, fold the paper this way.

30. WHAT ARE INDEFINITE AND NEGATIVE PRONOUNS?

An **indefinite pronoun** is a word used to refer to an unidentified person or thing. The term *indefinite* means "not definite," "undefined" (ex. *someone, anything*). A **negative pronoun** is the negative equivalent of an indefinite pronoun; it negates or denies the existence of someone or something (ex. *nobody, nothing*). See **What is a Pronoun?**, p. 7.

IN ENGLISH

Because each indefinite pronoun has a corresponding negative pronoun, it is helpful to study them in pairs. The most common pairs are:

Affirmative	Negative
referring to persons	
someone	no one
anyone	
somebody	nobody
anybody	
referring to things	
something	nothing
anything	

Use of Indefinite Pronouns in Questions and Answers

When asking a question, a speaker will use one of the affirmative pronouns: a pronoun starting with *some* if an affirmative answer is expected, or a pronoun starting with *any* if a negative answer is expected.

> Is *somebody* coming?
>> The speaker has a reason to believe that somebody may be coming.

> Is *anybody* coming?
>> The speaker has a reason to believe that nobody may be coming.

AFFIRMATIVE RESPONSE—You can respond affirmatively to questions containing an indefinite pronoun with the same indefinite pronoun (ex. *somebody*) or with the actual name of a person or a thing.

question   Is *somebody* (or *someone*) coming?
                  |
                  indefinite pronoun

answer 1   Yes, *somebody* (or *someone*) is coming.
                  |
                  indefinite pronoun

answer 2   Yes, *Jane* is coming.
                  |
                  actual name

NEGATIVE RESPONSE—To respond negatively, you must pay attention to the function of the indefinite pronoun. The indefinite pronoun used in the answer is different depending on whether it is the subject or has any other function in the answer.

- when an indefinite pronoun is the subject of a sentence there is only one way to respond negatively; i.e., with the corresponding negative pronoun.

question   Is *somebody* (or *someone*) coming?
                  |
                  indefinite pronoun → subject

answer   No, *nobody* (or *no one*) is coming.
                  |
                  negative pronoun → subject

- when an indefinite pronoun is anything other than the subject of a sentence, there are two ways to respond negatively:

1. negate the verb and keep the affirmative indefinite pronoun, or
2. keep the affirmative verb and use the corresponding negative pronoun.

It is important to use one way or the other and not to use both. The more common is to negate the verb.

question   Did you give it to *anybody?*
                  |_____| |
                       verb   indefinite pronoun → indirect object

answer 1   No, I *didn't* give it to *anybody.*
                       | |
                  verb negated   indefinite pronoun → indirect object

answer 2   No, I gave it to *nobody.*
                        | |
                       verb   negative pronoun → indirect object

question	Did he say *anything?*
	verb indefinite pronoun → direct object
answer 1	No, he *didn't* say *anything.*
	verb negated indefinite pronoun → direct object
answer 2	No, he said *nothing.*
	verb negative pronoun → direct object

IN JAPANESE

Just as in English, indefinite pronouns are used when the identity of a person or thing is unknown. Japanese indefinite pronouns are formed with interrogative pronouns and a particle.

INDEFINITE PRONOUNS—Indefinite pronouns are formed by attaching the particle **ka** to interrogative pronouns (see p. 103 in **What is an Interrogative Word?**). Since the particles **ga** indicating subject and **o** indicating direct object are often omitted with indefinite pronouns, we have indicated them between parentheses in the examples below.

Interrogative pronoun	→	Indefinite pronoun	
dare	*who*	dare**ka**	*someone, anyone*
nani	*what*	nani**ka**	*something, anything*

Dareka (ga) wakarimasu.
Someone can understand.

Nanika (o) tabemasu.
I'll eat something.

Although *somewhere, anywhere* and *sometime, anywhere* are adverbs in English, their Japanese equivalents take another part of speech. **Dokoka** *(somewhere, anywhere)* is a pronoun, and **itsuka** *(sometime, anytime)* can function either as a pronoun or an adverb.

Interrogative pronoun	→	Indefinite pronoun	
doko	*where*	doko**ka**	*somewhere, anywhere*
itsu	*when*	itsu**ka**	*sometime, anytime*

Dokoka e ikimasu.
I'll go somewhere.

Go-gatsu no **itsuka** ni narimasu.
It'll be sometime in May.

NEGATIVE PRONOUNS—Japanese does not have negative pronouns corresponding to *no one, nothing,* or the negative adverb *nowhere.* Instead, phrases consisting of interrogative pronouns followed by the particle **mo** are used in negative sentences. (One exception is **itsu** *(when)* + **mo,** which means *always* and not *(not) anytime.*)

Interrogative pronoun	→	Negative expression	
dare	*who*	dare **mo**	*no one, (not) anyone*
nani	*what*	nani **mo**	*nothing, (not) anything*
doko	*where*	doko e **mo**	*nowhere, (not) to any place*
doko	*where*	doko ni **mo**	*nowhere, (not) in any place*

Unlike the negative pronouns in English which must be used in affirmative sentences, in Japanese the negative indefinite expressions must be used in negative sentences.

Dare mo wakari**masen.**
   |
   verb negated "not understand"
No one understands.

Nani mo oishi**ku arimasen.**
   |
   i-type adjective negated "is not tasty"
Nothing is tasty.

Use of Indefinite Pronouns in Questions and Answers

Unlike English, there is no distinction in Japanese between a question using the indefinite pronouns *someone, somebody, something* and one using *anyone, anybody, anything.*

Is **somebody** coming?	[Implied: Somebody may be coming.]
Is **anybody** coming?	[Implied: Nobody may be coming.]

Dareka (ga) kimasu ka.

   |
   indefinite pronoun

AFFIRMATIVE RESPONSE—As in English, you can respond affirmatively to questions containing an indefinite pronoun with the same indefinite pronoun (ex. **dareka,** *somebody)* or with the actual name of a person or a thing.

question	**Dareka** (o) yobimasu ka.
	indefinite pronoun
	*Will you invite **somebody** (or **anybody**)?*
answer 1	Hai, **dareka** (o) yobimasu.
	indefinite pronoun
	*Yes, I will invite **somebody** (or **someone**).*
answer 2	Hai, **Suzuki-san** o yobimasu.
	actual name
	*Yes, I will invite **Ms. Suzuki**.*

NEGATIVE RESPONSE—There is only one way to respond negatively to questions which contain an indefinite pronoun. You must use interrogative pronouns + **mo** with a negative predicate.

question	**Dareka** (o) yobimasu ka.
	*Will you invite **somebody** (or **anybody**)?*
answer	Iie, **dare mo** yobi**masen**.
	verb negated "not invite"
	*No, I won't invite **anybody**.*
	*No, I will invite **nobody**.*

question	**Nanika** (ga) okashii desu ka.
	i-type adjective
	*Is **something** (or **anything**) funny?*
answer	Iie, **nani mo** okashi**ku arimasen**.
	i-type adjective negated "is not funny"
	*No, **nothing** is funny.*

To express the meaning *not anywhere, nowhere* in Japanese, an appropriate particle (the same particle used after the indefinite pronoun in the question) must be inserted between the pronoun **doko** *(where)* and the particle **mo**, as well as negating the verb.

question	**Dokoka e** ikimasu ka.
	some place to go
	*Are you going **somewhere** (or **anywhere**)?*
answer	Iie, **doko e mo** iki**masen**.
	no where to not go
	*No, I'm not going **anywhere**.*
	*No, I'm going **nowhere**.*

question	Resutoran wa **dokoka ni** arimasu ka.
	restaurant some place in there is

*Is there a restaurant **somewhere** (or **anywhere**)?*

answer	Iie, **doko ni mo** arimasen.
	no where in there isn't

*No, there isn't one **anywhere**.*

"Anyone, anything" Meaning "No matter who, no matter what"

IN ENGLISH
Anyone, anybody, anything, anywhere and *anytime* are not only used in negative sentences. They are also used in affirmative sentences expressing the meaning "no matter who it is, whoever," "no matter what it is, whatever," and so on.

Anybody can understand it.

No matter who it is, he or she can understand it.

She can understand *anything*.

No matter what it is, she can understand.

IN JAPANESE
To express *anybody, anyone, anything, anywhere* and *anytime* in the sense of "no matter who it is, whoever" and "no matter what it is, whatever," and so on, Japanese uses interrogative pronouns + **demo** in affirmative sentences.

Interrogative pronoun	→	Indefinite affirmative expression
dare	*who*	dare **demo** *anyone (no matter who)*
nani	*what*	nan **demo** *anything (no matter what)*
doko	*where*	doko **demo** *anywhere (no matter where)*
itsu	*when*	itsu **demo** *anytime (no matter when)*

Be sure not to confuse **dare demo** *(anyone)*, **nan demo** *(anything)*, etc. used in affirmative sentences, with **dare mo** *(anyone)*, **nani mo** *(anything)*, etc., used in negative sentences.

Dare demo dekimasu.

    verb "can do"

***Anyone** can do it.*

Dare mo dekimasen.

verb negated "cannot do"

No one can do it.

Summary

Here is a summary of English indefinite and negative pronouns and their Japanese equivalents.

INDEFINITE PRONOUN *(somebody, something)*
→ interrogative pronoun + **ka** in affirmative sentence

Dareka (ga) wakarimasu.

interrogative   verb in the
pronoun + **ka**   affirmative

Somebody understands.

Nanika (o) tabemasu.

interrogative   verb in the
pronoun + **ka**   affirmative

I'll eat something.

NEGATIVE PRONOUN *(nobody, nothing)*
→ interrogative pronoun + **mo** in negative sentence

Dare mo wakari**masen**.

interrogative   verb negated
pronoun + **mo**

Nobody understands.

Nani mo tabe**masen**.

interrogative   verb negated
pronoun + **mo**

I will eat nothing. (I won't eat anything.)

"ANYBODY, ANYTHING" *("no matter who, what," etc.)*
→ interrogative pronoun + **demo** in affirmative sentence

Dare demo wakarimasu.

interrogative   verb in the
pronoun + **demo**   affirmative

Anybody can understand it. [*Anybody* means "no matter who."]

Nan demo tabemasu.

interrogative   verb in the
pronoun **+ demo** affirmative

*I'll eat **anything***. [*Anything* means "no matter what."]

"One", "Ones"

There is another indefinite pronoun which we will examine separately because it does not follow the same pattern as those above.

IN ENGLISH

Like other indefinite pronouns, ***one*** in the singular form and ***ones*** in the plural form do not point out a specific person or thing. Unlike other indefinite pronouns, however, they are always modified by an adjective or a relative clause that helps us identify the person or thing by giving additional information (see **What is a Relative Clause?**, p. 177).

Which mugs do you prefer?
I prefer big *ones*.

    adjective

> The adjective *big* gives us additional information about *ones* (referring to *mugs*).

What book are you reading?
I'm reading the *one* that I bought yesterday.

        relative clause

> The relative clause *that I bought yesterday* gives us additional information about *one*, referring to *book*.

IN JAPANESE

The Japanese indefinite pronoun corresponding to *one* and *ones* is **no**, which is used for both singular and plural meanings. **No** must always be modified by a noun, an adjective or a relative clause. (Remember that in English, *one* and *ones* are never modified by a noun, only by an adjective or a relative clause.)

Kutsu o kaitai kedo, **Nihon no** wa chiisasugimasu.

    noun

> **Nihon** *(Japan)* gives us additional information about **no** *(one)*, referring to **kutsu** *(shoes)*.

*I want to buy shoes, but the **Japanese ones** are too small.*

Dono magu ga ii desu ka.—**Ookii no** ga ii desu.
adjective

Ookii *(big)* gives us additional information about **no** *(one)*, referring to **magu** *(mugs)*.

*Which mug(s) do you prefer?—I prefer a **big one** (or **big ones**).*

Dono hon o yonde imasu ka.—**Kinoo katta no** o yonde imasu.
relative clause

Kinoo katta *(bought yesterday)* gives us additional information about **no** *(one)*, referring to **hon** *(book)*.

*What book are you reading? I'm reading the **one I bought yesterday**.*

▼▼▼▼▼▼▼▼▼▼▼▼▼▼▼▼▼REVIEW▼▼▼▼▼▼▼▼▼▼▼▼▼▼▼▼▼

Circle the indefinite and negative pronouns in the following sentences.

1. I want somebody to help me with this project.

2. Nobody is free at the moment.

3. Do you care for anything to drink?—Nothing, thanks.

4. They will do anything to carry out their plans, won't they?

5. Anyone can do such a simple task in a minute.

31. What are Indefinite and Negative Adverbs?

An **indefinite adverb** is a word used to refer to the place, time, or purpose of an action when the speaker cannot or does not wish to be specific (ex. *anywhere, sometime*). A **negative adverb** is the negative equivalent of an indefinite adverb; it negates or denies the place, time, or purpose of an action (ex. *nowhere, never*). See **What is an Adverb?**, p. 40.

IN ENGLISH

Because each indefinite adverb has a corresponding negative adverb, it is helpful to study them in pairs.[1] The most common pairs are:

Affirmative	Negative
referring to location	
somewhere	nowhere
anywhere	
referring to time	
sometime	never
anytime	
ever	

Use of Indefinite Adverbs in Questions and Answers

There are two ways to ask questions with indefinite adverbs, either with *somewhere* and *sometime* or with *anywhere* and *anytime,* depending on the speaker's belief at the time.

> Are you going *somewhere?*
>
>> The speaker has reason to believe that the listener may be going somewhere.
>
> Are you going *anywhere?*
>
>> The speaker has reason to believe that the listener may not be going anywhere.

AFFIRMATIVE RESPONSE—You can respond affirmatively to questions containing an indefinite adverb with the same indefinite adverb (ex. *somewhere*) or with the actual name of a place or a specific time.

---

[1] What we have said about the use of indefinite and negative pronouns in English also applies to indefinite and negative adverbs (see p. 117).

question	Are you going *somewhere* ?
	indefinite adverb
answer 1	Yes, I'm going *somewhere.*
	indefinite adverb
answer 2	Yes, I'm going to *Florida.*
	name of a specific place

NEGATIVE RESPONSE—There are two ways to respond negatively to questions which contain indefinite adverbs:

1. negate the verb and keep the indefinite adverb, or

2. keep the affirmative verb and use the corresponding negative adverb

It is important to use one way or the other and not to use both. The more common is to negate the verb.

question	Is he going *anywhere?*
	indefinite adverb
answer 1	No, he *isn't* going *anywhere.*
	verb negated indefinite adverb
answer 2	No, he *is* going *nowhere.*
	verb negative adverb

question	Will you go to Japan *sometime?*
	indefinite adverb
answer 1	No, I *won't ever* go to Japan.
	indefinite adverb
	verb negated
answer 2	No, I'll *never* go to Japan.
	verb
	negative adverb

IN JAPANESE

Just as in English, Japanese indefinite adverbs are used when the place, time, or purpose of an action is unknown.

INDEFINITE ADVERBS—Indefinite adverbs are formed by attaching the particle **ka** to interrogative adverbs (see **What is an Interrogative Word?**, p. 102).[1] Here are some common indefinite adverbs.

Interrogative adverb	→	Indefinite adverb	
itsu	*when*	itsu**ka**	*some day, sometime, anytime*
dooshite	*why*	dooshite**ka**	*for some reason*
ikura	*how much*	ikura**ka**	*some, some amount*

> **Itsuka** ikimasu.
> *I'll go **sometime**.*

> Mise wa **dooshiteka** shimatte imasu.
> *The store is closed **for some reason**.*

> Okane wa **ikuraka** motte imasu.
> *I have **some** money.*

NEGATIVE ADVERBS—Japanese does not have negative adverbs corresponding to *nowhere* or *never*. Instead, adverbs such as **zenzen** *(at all)* and **zettai (ni)** *(absolutely)* can be used in negative sentences for emphasis.

> **Zenzen** wakari**masen**.
> |
>   verb negated
> *I **don't** understand **at all**.*

> Sonna koto wa **zettai ni** yari**masen**.
> |
>   verb negated
> *I'll **never** do such a thing.*

Use of Indefinite Adverbs in Questions and Answers

AFFIRMATIVE RESPONSE—As in English, you can respond affirmatively to questions containing an indefinite adverb with the same indefinite adverb (ex. **itsuka,** *sometime*) or with an actual time (ex. **rainen,** *next year*).

> question   **Itsuka** Nihon e ikimasu ka.
> |
>   indefinite adverb
>   *Will you go to Japan **sometime**?*

---

[1] For the most part, what we have said about the indefinite and negative pronouns in Japanese also applies to indefinite and negative adverbs (see p. 119).

answer 1	Hai, **itsuka** ikimasu.

indefinite adverb

Yes, I'll go sometime.

answer 2	Hai, **rainen** ikimasu.

actual time

Yes, I'm going next year.

NEGATIVE RESPONSE—To respond negatively to questions which contain an indefinite adverb, it is sufficient to use a negative sentence without an adverb. However, for emphasis you can add an adverb such as **zenzen** *(at all)*.

question	Okane wa **ikuraka** arimasu ka.

indefinite adverb

Is there some (or any) money?

answer 1	Iie, ari**masen**.

verb negated "there isn't"

No, there isn't.

answer 2	Iie, **zenzen** ari**masen**.

adverb   verb negated "there isn't"

No, there isn't at all.

"Anywhere, Anytime" Meaning "No matter where, No matter when"

IN ENGLISH
In addition to their use in questions and negative sentences, the indefinite adverbs *anywhere* and *anytime* can be used in affirmative sentences expressing the meaning "no matter where it is, wherever" and "no matter when it is, whenever," respectively.

They would go *anywhere*.
No matter where it is, they would go.

Come and visit us *anytime*.
No matter when it is, come and visit us.

IN JAPANESE
Corresponding to the English indefinite adverbs *anytime* and *any amount* in the sense of "no matter when it is, whenever" and "no matter how much it is, however much," Japanese uses interrogative adverbs + **demo** in affirmative sentences.

adverb		→	**Indefinite adverb**	
itsu	*when*		itsu **demo**	*anytime, no matter when, whenever*
ikura	*how much*		ikura **demo**	*any amount, no matter how much, however much*

Itsu demo asobi ni kite kudasai.
*Come and visit us **anytime**.*

Okane wa **ikura demo** kashite agemasu.
*I'll lend you **any amount** of money.*
***No matter how much** money, I'll lend it to you.*

Summary

Here is a summary of English indefinite and negative adverbs and their Japanese equivalents.

INDEFINITE AFFIRMATIVE ADVERB *(some day, for some reason, some amount)*
→ interrogative adverb + **ka** in affirmative sentence

Itsuka Yooroppa e ikitai desu.

interrogative   verb in the
adverb + **ka**   affirmative

*I want to go to Europe **some day**.*

INDEFINITE ADVERB *(nowhere, never)*
→ use adverbs such as **zenzen** *(at all)* and **zettai (ni)** *(absolutely)* in negative sentence

Ano ko wa **zenzen** benkyoo shi**masen**.

      adverb   verb negated

*That child doesn't study **at all**.*

"ANYTIME, ANY AMOUNT" *("no matter when, no matter how much")*
→ interrogative adverb + **demo** in affirmative sentence

Ikura demo tsukatte kudasai.

interrogative   verb in the
adverb + **demo** affirmative

*Please use it **as much as you want (any amount)**.*
[*any amount* means "no matter how much"]

▼▼▼▼▼▼▼▼▼▼▼▼▼▼▼▼REVIEW▼▼▼▼▼▼▼▼▼▼▼▼▼▼▼▼

Circle the indefinite and negative adverbs in the following sentences.

1. Shall we go somewhere for a vacation?
2. I'm so busy that I can't go anywhere.
3. At this rate I'll never be able to finish my paper.
4. If you keep working at it, you'll finish it sometime.
5. Come and ask me anytime if you have questions.
6. I'm afraid he'll go nowhere with that kind of plan.

32. What is Meant by Tense?

The **tense** of a sentence indicates the time when the action of the verb takes place or the time when the description expressed by a noun or an adjective is true (at the present time, in the past, or in the future).

IN ENGLISH
The tense of the sentence is indicated by the verb form.

present	I eat.
past	I ate.
future	I will eat.

As you can see in the above examples, just by putting the verb in a different tense and without giving any additional information, you can indicate when the action of the verb takes place. The tense of the verb can be emphasized by the use of adverbs, such as "I eat *every day*," "I ate *yesterday*," and "I will eat *tomorrow*."

Tenses may be classified according to the way they are formed. A **simple tense** consists of only one verb form, while a **compound tense** consists of two or more verb forms.

I *eat.*
simple tense

I *am eating.*
compound tense

Listed below are the main English tenses. There are only two simple tenses: the present (ex. I *study*) and the past (ex. I *studied*). All of the other tenses are compound tenses formed by one or more auxiliary verbs plus the main verb (see **What is an Auxiliary Verb?**, p. 31).

PRESENT

present	I study
present progressive	I am studying

PAST

simple past	I studied
past progressive	I was studying
present perfect	I have studied
past perfect	I had studied

FUTURE

future	I will study
future progressive	I will be studying
future perfect	I will have studied

You will find more details on the various tenses in **What is the Present Tense?**, p. 136, **What is the Past Tense?**, p. 142, and **What is the Future Tense?**, p. 139, and **What is the Progressive?**, p.146.

IN JAPANESE

Tense is indicated by a suffix attached to the main predicate, which always appears at the end of a sentence. Unlike English, where the main predicate is always a verb, the main predicate in Japanese can be a verb, the copula, or an **i**-type adjective. (See **What are Prefixes and Suffixes?**, p. 53, **What are the Uses of the Verb "To be"?**, p. 26, and **What is a Descriptive Adjective?**, p. 36).

Here are some examples of sentences in the polite style in which the tense is indicated in a variety of ways: the verb, the copula and the **i**-type adjective. (See **What is Meant by Polite and Plain Forms?**, p. 57, and for plain style forms refer to your textbook.)

Yamada-san wa maiban **dekakemasu**.
Mr. Yamada   every night   go out
                                          |
                            tense indicated on the verb

*Mr. Yamada **goes out** every night.*

Yamada-san wa kaisha-in **desu**.
Mr. Yamada   company   is
                        employee |
                            tense indicated on the copula

*Mr. Yamada **is** a company employee.*

Yamada-san wa **isogashii** desu.
Mr. Yamada   is busy |
                        | polite marker
              tense indicated on the **i**-type adjective

*Mr. Yamada **is busy**.*

Unlike the many tenses in English, Japanese has only two tenses: the nonpast, corresponding to the English present and future, and the past, corresponding to the English past. Both are simple tenses.

Make sure that you identify whether the main predicate (verb, copula or i-type adjective) is in a main or subordinate clause since the tense will be expressed differently depending on the type of clause (see **What are the Different Types of Sentences and Clauses?**, p. 167).

When you want to indicate tense, it may be helpful to ask yourself the following questions in order to choose the correct Japanese form:

1. Is the polite or plain style appropriate?
2. Should the tense be indicated by a verb, a copula or an i-type adjective?
3. Is the nonpast or a past tense required?
4. Is the sentence affirmative or negative?
5. Is the clause a main clause or a subordinate clause?

Let us take the following as an example of a sentence that you want to express in Japanese. Suppose that you are talking to a new Japanese teacher.

> *I went to Japan last summer.*
>
>   1. Style: Polite
>   2. Tense indicated by: verb
>   3. Nonpast or past: past
>   4. Affirmative or negative: affirmative
>   5. Clause: main clause (There is only one clause.)

The Japanese equivalent will be the following (the subject **watashi** *(I)* along with its particle **wa** can be omitted):

> (Watashi wa) kyonen no natsu Nihon e **ikimashita**.
>   I   last year   's summer Japan to   went

▼▼▼▼▼▼▼▼▼▼▼▼▼▼▼▼▼REVIEW▼▼▼▼▼▼▼▼▼▼▼▼▼▼▼▼▼

I. Fill in the blanks.

The word tense refers to the (1) _____ when an action takes place. A (2) _____ tense consists of one verb form; a compound tense consists of (3) _____ or more verb forms: an (4) _____ verb (or verbs) plus the (5) _____ verb. The (6) _____ and (7) _____ tenses are examples of two simple tenses in English. Japanese has nonpast and (8) _____ tenses. The nonpast tense expresses both present and (9) _____.

II. Indicate the tense of the English verb at the end of each sentence: Past (P), Present (PR) or Future (F).
- Indicate the appropriate Japanese tense for each verb: Past (P) or Non past (NP).

1. I enjoy riding my bicycle to school.   P   PR   F

→ equivalent sentence in Japanese   P   NP

2. My parents visited Spain last summer.   P   PR   F

→ equivalent sentence in Japanese   P   NP

3. The dentist's office will call you next week.   P   PR   F

→ equivalent sentence in Japanese   P   NP

33. WHAT IS THE PRESENT TENSE?

The **present tense** indicates that the action expressed by a verb is happening at the present time or that the description expressed by a noun or an adjective is true at the present time. It can be:

- when the speaker is speaking   I *see* you.
- a habitual action   He *swims* when he has time.
- a general truth   The earth *is* round.

IN ENGLISH

There are three forms of the verb which indicate the present tense, although they have slightly different meanings.

present	Paul *studies* in the library.
present progressive	Paul *is studying* in the library.
present emphatic	Paul *does study* in the library.

When you answer the following questions, you will automatically choose one of the above forms.

> Where does Paul study? Paul *studies* in the library.
> Where is Paul now? Paul *is studying* in the library.
> Does Paul ever study? Yes, Paul *does study*.

IN JAPANESE

The present tense is indicated by the **nonpast** form of a verb, the copula or an **i**-type adjective. The nonpast tense has both polite and plain forms, as well as affirmative and negative forms in each style (see **What is Meant by Polite and Plain Forms?**, p. 57, and **What are Affirmative and Negative Sentences?**, p. 92).

Here are examples of nonpast tense forms of a verb, the copula and an **i**-type adjective in the polite style. (For tenses indicated in the plain style, see your textbook.)

VERBS

PRESENT TENSE	affirmative:	-masu
	negative:	-masen

> Hayashi-san wa niku o **tabe*masu***.
> |
>   present affirmative
> *Ms. Hayashi **eats** meat.*

Mori-san wa niku o **tabe*masen***.

present negative

*Ms. Mori **does not eat** meat.*

Japanese has no equivalent of the English present emphatic (ex. *I do believe, He does study)*; make sure that you ignore this kind of *do* and *does* when you are using Japanese.

COPULA

PRESENT TENSE	affirmative:	desu
	negative:	dewa arimasen
	or	ja arimasen

Kyoo wa yasumi **desu**.

present affirmative

*Today **is** a holiday.*

Suiyoobi wa yasumi **dewa** (*or* **ja**) **arimasen**.

present negative

*Wednesday **is not** a holiday.*

i-TYPE ADJECTIVE

PRESENT TENSE	affirmative:	-i desu
	negative:	-ku arimasen
	or	-ku nai desu

Sushi wa oish**ii** *desu*.

present affirmative

*Sushi **is delicious**.*

Tenpura wa **oishi*ku* arimasen** (*or* **oishi*ku* nai desu**).

present negative

*Tenpura **is not delicious**.*

Present or Future?

The nonpast tense includes both the present and the future. You can interpret it as indicating the present or future tense by the context or by the adverbs in a sentence, such as **mainichi** *(every day* → present) and **ashita** *(tomorrow* → future).

Suzuki-san wa **maishuu** yakyuu o **yari*masu***.
Mr. Suzuki   every week baseball   plays
               | |
            adverb   present tense
Mr. Suzuki plays baseball every week.

Nakamura-san wa **amari** yakyuu o **yari*masen***.
Mr. Nakamura does not play baseball often.

Suzuki-san wa **ashita** yakyuu o **yari*masu***.
Mr. Suzuki   tomorrow baseball   will play
               | |
            adverb   future tense
Mr. Suzuki will play baseball tomorrow.

Nakamura-san wa **ashita** yakyuu o **yari*masen***.
Mr. Nakamura will not play baseball tomorrow.

▼▼▼▼▼▼▼▼▼▼▼▼▼▼▼▼▼REVIEW▼▼▼▼▼▼▼▼▼▼▼▼▼▼▼▼▼

I. Fill in the blanks.

The present tense is expressed by the nonpast tense in Japanese. In the nonpast tense a polite-style verb ends in (1) _____ in the affirmative and in (2) _____ in the negative. The nonpast form of the copula in the polite style is (3) _____ in the affirmative and (4) _____ or (5) _____ in the negative, while the nonpast form of an **i**-type adjective ends in (6) _____ in the affirmative and (7) _____ or (8) _____ in the negative.

II. For each pair, indicate whether, in Japanese, the italicized words will be indicated by the "Same" or "Different" forms of the verb.

1. We *vote* every year.

   We *will vote* tomorrow.   SAME   DIFFERENT

2. Kazuko *takes* the bus to work.

   Kazuko *doesn't take* the bus to work.   SAME   DIFFERENT

3. The door *opens* automatically.

   The door *opened* automatically.   SAME   DIFFERENT

34. WHAT IS THE FUTURE TENSE?

The **future tense** indicates that the action expressed by a verb will take place some time in the future or that the description expressed by a noun or an adjective will be true at a future time.

IN ENGLISH
The future tense of a sentence can only be expressed by the verb. The verb form for the future is *will* or *shall* + the dictionary form of the main verb. *Shall* is used in formal English, while *will* occurs in everyday language.

> I *will clean* my room tomorrow.
> Naomi *will leave* tonight.

In conversation, *shall* and *will* are often shortened to *'ll*.

> I*'ll clean* my room tomorrow.
> She*'ll leave* tonight.

IN JAPANESE
The future tense is indicated by the nonpast form of a verb, the copula or an **i**-type adjective. Since the nonpast is also used for the present tense, the forms are the same as the ones discussed in **What is the Present Tense?**, p. 136. You can usually tell by the context when the Japanese nonpast expresses the future tense and not the present tense, especially if there are words that indicate time, such as **ashita** *(tomorrow)* and **raishuu** *(next week)*.

The future tense has both polite style and plain style forms, as well as affirmative and negative forms in each style (see **What is Meant by Polite and Plain Forms?**, p. 57, and **What are Affirmative and Negative Sentences?**, p. 92).

Here are examples of future tense forms of a verb, the copula and an **i**-type adjective in the polite style. (For tenses indicated in the plain style, consult your textbook.)

VERB

FUTURE TENSE	affirmative:	-masu
	negative:	-masen

Suzuki-san wa **ashita** kaisha e **ikimasu**.
Mr. Suzuki   tomorrow work   to   will go
             | |
           adverb   future affirmative
Mr. Suzuki **will go** *to work* **tomorrow.**

Tanaka-san wa **ashita** kaisha e **iki*masen***.
Mr. Tanaka   tomorrow work to will not go
                     | |
          adverb   future negative

*Mr. Tanaka **will not go** to work **tomorrow**.*

COPULA

FUTURE TENSE   **affirmative:**   particle **ni** + the verb **narimasu** *(become)*
                 negative: particle **ni** + the verb **narimasen** *(not become)*
(In some cases the nonpast tense form **desu** *(is)* and **dewa** (or **ja**) **arimasen** *(is not)* can be used. Refer to your textbook.)

Watashi wa isha **ni narimasu**.
    I   doctor   will be(come)
             | |
          noun   future affirmative

*I **will be(come)** a doctor.*

Otooto wa isha **ni narimasen**.
brother   doctor   won't be(come)
          | |
       noun   future negative

*My brother **will not be(come)** a doctor.*

I-TYPE ADJECIVE

FUTURE TENSE   **affirmative:**   **-ku** + the verb **narimasu** *(become)*
                 negative: **-ku** + the verb **narimasen** *(not become)*
(In some cases the nonpast tense form **-i desu** *(is)* and **-ku arimasen** or **-ku nai desu** *(is not)* can be used. Refer to your textbook.)

Ashita wa **atsu*ku narimasu***.
tomorrow   hot   will be(come)
            | |
     i-type adj. future affirmative

*It **will be(come)** hot tomorrow.*

Konban wa **atsu*ku narimasen***.
tonight   hot   won't be(come)
          | |
     i-type adj.   future negative

*It **will not be(come)** hot tonight.*

Alternate Ways to Express the Future

IN ENGLISH

Besides using the future tense itself, there are two ways to express an action which will occur some time in the future.

One way is to use the verb *to go* in the present progressive + the dictionary form of the main verb: *I am going to read, she is going to sing,* etc. (See **What is the Progressive?**, p. 146.)

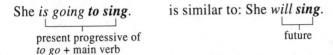

She *is going to sing.*   is similar to: She *will sing.*

present progressive of   future
to go + main verb

Another way to express an immediate future is to use the present progressive form of verbs, especially those indicating an arrival and departure. The two sentences in each of the following pairs are similar in meaning.

> I*'m going* out tonight.
> I *will go* out tonight.

> My parents *are coming* on Friday.
> My parents *will come* on Friday.

IN JAPANESE
There is no equivalent of the construction *going to* + the main verb nor can the Japanese present progressive construction be used to indicate actions which are going to happen in the near future. Do not try to use these English constructions directly in Japanese, simply use the future (i.e. nonpast) form.

▼▼▼▼▼▼▼▼▼▼▼▼▼▼▼▼REVIEW▼▼▼▼▼▼▼▼▼▼▼▼▼▼▼▼

Fill in the blanks.

In Japanese the future tense of a verb is expressed by the nonpast form, which is the same form as the (1) _____ tense. In the future tense a polite style verb ends in (2) _____ in the affirmative and in (3) _____ in the negative. The future tense form of the copula is (4) _____ + **narimasu** in the affirmative and (5) _____ + **narimasen** in the negative, while the future tense form of an **i**-type adjective is (6) _____ + **narimasu** in the affirmative and (7) _____ + **narimasen** in the negative.

35. WHAT IS THE PAST TENSE?

The **past tense** indicates that the action expressed by the verb occurred in the past or that the description expressed by a noun or an adjective was true in the past.

IN ENGLISH
The past tense of a sentence can only be expressed by the verb. There are several verb forms that indicate that the action took place in the past.

simple past	I worked
past progressive	I was working
with the auxiliary verb used to	I used to work
past emphatic	I did work
present perfect	I have worked
past perfect	I had worked

The simple past is called "simple" because it is a simple tense; i.e., it consists of one word (*worked* in the example above). The other past tenses are compound tenses; i.e., they consist of more than one word (*was working, did work,* etc.). The past progressive is discussed in a separate section (see **What is the Progressive?**, p. 146).

IN JAPANESE
The past tense is indicated by the past form of a verb, the copula, or an **i**-type adjective. The past tense has both polite and plain forms, as well as affirmative and negative forms in each style (see **What is Meant by Polite and Plain Forms?**, p. 57, and **What are Affirmative and Negative Sentences?**, p. 92).

Here are examples of past tense forms of a verb, the copula and an **i**-type adjective in the polite style. (For tenses indicated in the plain style, consult your textbook.)

VERB

PAST TENSE   affirmative: **-mashita**
              negative: **-masendeshita**

Honda-san wa denwa o **kake*mashita***.
                                 past affirmative form
*Ms. Honda **made** a phone call.*

Matsuda-san wa denwa o **kake*masendeshita*.**

past negative form

*Ms. Matsuda **did not make** a phone call.*

In the case of certain verbs, the affirmative **mashita** ending can also express the **present perfect** *(has done...)*. You can usually tell by the context that it is a present perfect and not a simple past, especially if there are adverbs such as **moo** *(already)*.

simple past in the affirmative
Honda-san wa kinoo **kaeri*mashita*.**
Ms. Honda   yesterday   returned

past affirmative

*Ms. Honda **returned** yesterday.*

present perfect in the affirmative
Honda-san wa *moo* **kaeri*mashita*.**
Ms. Honda   already has returned

adverb   past affirmative

*Ms. Honda **has already returned**.*

To express the present perfect in the negative *(hasn't done...)*, the non-past **-masen** ending or the **te** form of the verb (p. 64) + the auxiliary verb **imasen** must be used (see **What is an Auxiliary Verb?**, p. 31). You cannot use the past negative form **-masendeshita** here.

simple past in the negative
Honda-san wa kinoo **kaeri*masendeshita*.**
Ms. Honda   yesterday   didn't return

adverb   past negative

*Ms. Honda **didn't return** yesterday.*

present perfect in the negative
Honda-san wa **mada kaeri*masen*.**
Ms. Honda   yet   hasn't returned

adverb   nonpast negative

*Ms. Honda **hasn't returned yet**.*

Honda-san wa **mada kaet*te imasen*.**
Ms. Honda   yet | hasn't returned

adverb   **te** form

*Mr. Honda **hasn't returned yet**.*

Japanese has no equivalent of the English past emphatic (ex. *I did work)*; make sure that in Japanese you ignore *did* in this type of construction.

COPULA

PAST TENSE	affirmative:	deshita
	negative:	dewa arimasendeshita
	or	ja arimasendeshita

Otera wa shizuka **deshita.**

             past affirmative

*The temple **was** quiet.*

Oshiro wa shizuka **dewa** (*or* **ja**) **arimasendeshita.**

                     past negative

*The castle **was not** quiet.*

I-TYPE ADJECTIVE

PAST TENSE	affirmative:	-katta desu
	negative:	-ku arimasendeshita
	or	-ku nakatta desu

Koogi wa **muzukashi*katta desu*.**

          past affirmative

*The lecture **was difficult.***

Shiken wa **muzukashi*ku arimasendeshita*.**
     (*or* **muzukashi*ku nakatta desu*.**)

             past negative

*The exam **was not difficult.***

▼▼▼▼▼▼▼▼▼▼▼▼▼▼▼▼REVIEW▼▼▼▼▼▼▼▼▼▼▼▼▼▼▼▼

I. Fill in the blanks.

The past tense is expressed by the past tense forms in Japanese. In the past tense a polite-style verb ends in (1) _____ in the affirmative and in (2) _____ in the negative. The polite-style past form of the copula is (3) _____ in the affirmative and (4) _____ or (5) _____ in the negative. The past form of an **i**-type adjective ends in (6) _____ in the affirmative and (7) _____ or (8) _____ in the negative.

II. Will the italicized parts of the sentences in each pair be indicated by the same form or different forms of verbs in Japanese? Circle "Same" or "Different" at the end of each pair.

1. Michio *studied* in the library.

   Michio *didn't study* in the library.   SAME   DIFFERENT

2. The train *arrived* ten minutes ago.

   The train *has* already *arrived*.   SAME   DIFFERENT

3. I *didn't eat* yesterday.

   I *haven't eaten* all day.   SAME   DIFFERENT

36. WHAT IS THE PROGRESSIVE?

The **progressive** construction is used to talk about actions or events that are in progress at a specific moment in time; they emphasize the moment that an action or event takes place.

> Kazuko *is talking* on the phone. [Right now.]
> We *were changing* the tires. [At that moment in the past.]

The progressive construction can be in the present, past or future tense.

present tense   It *is snowing*.
[Right now as I speak.]

past tense   It *was snowing*.
[At that moment; ex. when we arrived in Denver yesterday.]

future tense   It *will be snowing*.
[At that moment; ex. when we arrive in Denver tomorrow.]

IN ENGLISH

The progressive construction is made up of the auxiliary verb *to be* + the **present participle**, that is, the *-ing* form of the main verb. The tense of the auxiliary verb *to be* indicates when the action of the main verb takes place.

> We *are eating* right now.
> present tense / present participle
> of *to be*

> At that moment George *was watching* football on television.
> past tense   present participle
> of *to be*

> I *will be working* in the garden this afternoon.
> future tense   present participle
> of *to be*

In addition to describing an action happening at a specific moment, the progressive construction can be used to describe habitual actions.

> Mary *is working* right now, but she will be back soon.
> *Is working* describes what Mary is doing right at this moment.

Mary *is working* for a bank these days.

Is working describes where Mary works in general over a period of
time, not necessarily at this moment.

IN JAPANESE

The progressive construction is made up of the **te** form of the main
verb + the auxiliary verb **imasu** (see **What is an Auxiliary Verb?**,
p. 31). Consult your textbook for the formation of the **te** form. There
is no participle in Japanese.

The auxiliary verb **imasu** is placed at the end of a sentence, indicating
the style (plain or polite), tense (nonpast or past), and affirmative-negative distinction of the sentence. (The **te** form of a verb literally means
"*do... and,*"and does not indicate tense.)

▪ in the nonpast tense

Ima koko de Miki-san o **matte imasu**.
now   here at Miki   waiting   am
                              | |
                           te form nonpast tense

I am waiting for Miki here now.
└──┬──┘
present tense

Ashita san-ji ni koko de Miki-san o **matte imasu**.
tomorrow three at here   at Miki   waiting   am
                                         | |
                                      te form   nonpast tense

I will be waiting for Miki here at three (o'clock) tomorrow.
└────┬────┘
future tense

▪ in the past tense

Kinoo san-ji ni koko de Miki-san o **matte imashita**.
yesterday three at here   at Miki   waiting   was
                                         | |
                                      te form   past tense

I was waiting for Miki here at three (o'clock) yesterday.
└───┬───┘
past tense

As in English, the Japanese progressive construction is sometimes
used to describe habitual actions.

Emiko-san wa **saikin** ginkoo de **hataraite imasu**.
Emiko   these days bank for   working   is

Emiko is working for a bank these days.

Emiko-san wa **ima hataraite imasu** ga, sugu kaette kimasu.
Emiko   now working   is but soon return will come
*Emiko **is working** right **now**, but she will be back soon.*

Careful

1. Some sentences in the progressive construction in English should not be expressed with the progressive construction in Japanese. This is particularly true with verbs that have to do with coming and going in the progressive tense in English *(I am going, we are coming)*. For example:

Ima suupaa e **ikimasu**.
nonpast form indicating the future tense
*He (or she) **will go** to the supermarket now.*

or

Ima suupaa e **iku tokoro desu**.
a construction expressing *to be about to do*
*He (or she) **is about to go** to the supermarket now.*

and not as:

Ima suupaa e **itte imasu**.
a construction expressing a resultant state
*He (or she) **has gone** to the supermarket and **is still there**.*

The reason for this difference in meaning is that the **te** form + **imasu** construction also expresses a meaning other than the progressive meaning, that is, that the resultant state of an action still continues. Hence, in the sentence above, it would imply not only that the person has gone to the supermarket, but that the person is still there. That is not the meaning of the English sentence above.

2. Do not assume that all verbs ending in *-ing* in English function as present participles and, therefore, that you are dealing with a progressive tense. A verb often appears in the *-ing* form so that it can function as a noun and be a subject or an object of a sentence. When a verb functions as a noun in this way it is called a **gerund**.

Smoking is bad for your health.
|
gerund
    Smoking functions as a noun, and as subject of this sentence.

There is no gerund in Japanese. A word such as *smoking* in the above example will be translated by the plain form of a verb + **no**.

Tabako o **suu no** wa karada ni warui desu.
cigarettes   smoke   body   for is bad
      └──┬──┘

    plain form verb + **no**
    Tabako o suu no functions as a noun, and as subject of this sentence.
    Smoking cigarettes is bad for your health.

This type of **no** turns the preceding verb into a noun, just as adding *-ing* to the end of a verb does in English. In order to choose the correct Japanese equivalent, it is very important that you distinguish an English verb ending in *-ing* that functions as a present participle from one functioning as a noun.

▼▼▼▼▼▼▼▼▼▼▼▼▼▼▼▼▼▼**REVIEW**▼▼▼▼▼▼▼▼▼▼▼▼▼▼▼▼▼▼

Will the following English sentences be translated into the progressive construction in Japanese? Circle "Yes" or "No".

1. I was sleeping when you called me this morning.   Yes   No

2. My father is teaching at a high school.   Yes   No

3. Chris is returning on the next flight.   Yes   No

4. Look! It's snowing.   Yes   No

5. I enjoy watching old movies.   Yes   No

37. WHAT IS THE IMPERATIVE?

The **imperative** is the command form of a verb. It is used to give someone an order. There are affirmative commands (an order to do something) and negative commands (an order not to do something).

IN ENGLISH

There are two types of commands.

The *you*-**command** is used when giving an order to others. The dictionary form of the verb is used for the *you*-command.

Affirmative	→	Negative
Answer the phone.		*Don't answer* the phone.
Use this door.		*Don't use* this door.
Speak loudly.		*Don't speak* loudly.

Notice that the pronoun "you" is not stated. The absence of the pronoun *you* in the sentence is a good indication that you are dealing with an imperative and not a present tense.

The *we*-**command** is used when the speaker gives a suggestion to himself or herself as well as to others. In English this form begins with the phrase "let us" (often shortened as "let's") followed by the dictionary form of the verb.

Affirmative	→	Negative
Let us leave.		*Let us not leave.*
Let's go to the movies.		*Let's not go* to the movies.

IN JAPANESE

As in English, there are two basic types of commands, the *you*-command and the *we*-command. Each type has both a plain and a polite form (see **What is Meant by Polite and Plain Forms?**, p. 57). The plain *you*-command has both an affirmative (*"Do...!"*) and a negative (*"Don't...!"*) form, but other command expressions have only affirmative forms.

To express the meaning of a negative command other than in the plain *you*-command, Japanese uses the form "Quit doing..." or "Let's quit doing... ." Consult your textbook for these forms and the formation of all the command forms.

Use of the Various Command Forms

PLAIN *YOU*-COMMAND FORM—Only male speakers use this form and only to someone equal or lower in status, for example, to their close friends, children and younger siblings. The particle **yo** is usually added at the end of the sentence to soften the harsh tone. Students of Japanese must be careful about when to use this form as it sounds familiar and rude even with **yo**.

Affirmative	Negative
Chotto **mate** (**yo**).	Soko de **matsuna** (**yo**).
Wait a minute.	*Don't wait there.*
Koko ni **koi** (**yo**).	Koko ni **kuruna** (**yo**).
Come here.	*Don't come here.*

POLITE *YOU*-COMMAND FORM—Both men and women can use this form, but only to someone equal or lower in status, for example, to their close friends, children and younger siblings. Although it sounds less harsh than the plain *you*-command form, it still sounds familiar, and is considered rude when used to the wrong people. The particle **yo** or **ne** is often added at the end of the sentence.

Chotto **machinasai** (**yo** *or* **ne**).
Wait a minute.

Koko ni ki**nasai** (**yo** *or* **ne**).
Come here.

Speaking to someone equal in status, women usually use a shortened request form, namely, the **te** form of verbs (with or without **yo** or **ne**), instead of either of the *you*-command forms.

Chotto **matte** (**yo** *or* **ne**).
Wait a minute.

Koko ni **kite** (**yo** *or* **ne**).
Come here.

PLAIN *WE*-COMMAND FORM (also called the **oo form** or the **volitional form**)—Men use this form in informal situations speaking with someone equal or lower in status. In recent years, however, it has become more and more common for young women to use this form. The particle **yo** or **ne** is sometimes added at the end of the sentence to show the speaker's eagerness or to soften the tone.

Sukii ni **ikoo** (**yo** *or* **ne**).
Let's go skiing.

Nanika **tabeyoo** (**yo** *or* **ne**).
Let's eat something.

POLITE *WE*-COMMAND FORM—Both men and women use this form when they are speaking politely. In women's speech the particle **yo** or **ne** is sometimes added at the end of the sentence.

Kekkon **shimashoo** (**yo** *or* **ne**).
Let's get married.

▼▼▼▼▼▼▼▼▼▼▼▼▼▼▼▼REVIEW▼▼▼▼▼▼▼▼▼▼▼▼▼▼▼▼

I. Change the following sentences to the imperative affirmative.

1. You should practice the piano every day.

_____

2. We take a bus tour.

_____

II. Indicate if the Japanese verb in the sentence below is in the imperative (IMP) or nonpast (NP) tense.

1. Shinbun o yomoo.	IMP	NP
2. Okinasai.	IMP	NP
3. Dekakemasu.	IMP	NP
4. Tomaru.	IMP	NP
5. Kaerimashoo.	IMP	NP

38. WHAT IS MEANT BY ACTIVE AND PASSIVE VOICE?

The voice of the verb refers to a basic relationship between the verb and its subject. There are two voices: the active and the passive.

The **active voice**—A sentence is said to be in the active voice when the subject is the performer of the verb. In this instance, the verb is called an **active verb**. In the examples below, the subject (S) performs the action of the verb (V) and the direct object (DO) is the receiver of the action.

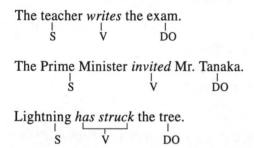

The passive **voice**—A sentence is said to be in the passive voice when the subject is the receiver of the action. In this instance, the verb is called a **passive verb**. In the examples below, the subject is having the action of the verb performed upon it. The performer of the action, called the **agent,** if it is mentioned, is introduced by the word *by.*

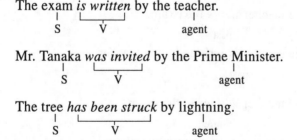

IN ENGLISH

The passive voice is expressed by a form of the verb *to be* + the main verb in what is called the past participle form.

The exam *is written* by the teacher.
        | |
   verb *to be*   past participle of the main verb *write*

Active Sentence → Passive Sentence

When an active sentence is changed into a passive sentence the following changes occur.

1. The direct or indirect object of the active sentence becomes the subject of the passive sentence.

active   Everyone makes *suggestions.*
                                                    |
                                            direct object

passive   *Suggestions* are made by everyone.
                      |
                subject

active   Paul gave a rose to *Liz.*
                                                    |
                                        indirect object

passive   *Liz* was given a rose by Paul.
                 |
               subject

2. The tense of the verb of the active sentence is reflected in the tense of the verb *to be* in the passive sentence.

active   The teacher *writes* the exam.
                                    |
                                present

passive   The exam *is* written by the teacher.
                              |
                          present

active   The teacher *wrote* the exam.
                                    |
                                past

passive   The exam *was* written by the teacher.
                              |
                            past

active   The teacher *will write* the exam.
                                        |
                                    future

passive   The exam *will be* written by the teacher.
                                  |
                              future

3. The subject of the active sentence becomes the agent of the passive sentence introduced with *by.* The agent is often omitted.

active   *The teacher* writes the exam.
                      |
                  subject

passive   The exam is written *by the teacher.*
                                    |
                                  agent

IN JAPANESE

As in English, a sentence is said to be in the passive voice when the subject is the receiver, instead of the performer, of the action. Below are the general guidelines to change an active sentence to a passive.

1. Verbs have a specific passive form. A verb in the active voice is made passive with the addition of the suffix **areru** or **rareru**. The choice between the two suffixes depends on which group the verb belongs to: **u** verbs, **ru** verbs, or irregular verbs (see **What is a Verb?**, p. 21). A passive verb, like any other verb, has a plain or polite form and an affirmative and negative form. (see **What is Meant by Polite and Plain Forms?**, p. 57).

Here is an example of an active and a passive sentence in the polite affirmative.

active   Shushoo wa Tanaka-san o **yobimashita**.
             Prime Minister Mr. Tanaka   invited
                                             |
                                        active verb
   *The Prime Minister **invited** Mr. Tanaka.*

passive   Tanaka-san wa Shushoo ni **yobaremashita**.
              Mr. Tanaka   Prime Min. by   was invited
                                                |
                                          passive verb
   *Mr. Tanaka **was invited** by the Prime Minister.*

2. The subject of the active sentence (marked with **wa** or **ga**) becomes the agent of the passive sentence followed by **ni**. As in English, the agent is often omitted.

active   **Shushoo wa** (*or* ga) Tanaka-san o yobimashita.
                  |
              subject
   The Prime Minister invited Mr. Tanaka.

passive   Tanaka-san wa **Shushoo ni** yobaremashita.
                                  |
                               agent
   *Mr. Tanaka was invited **by the Prime Minister**.*

3. The tense of the passive sentence is indicated at the end of the verb just as in the active sentence. The present and future tenses are expressed by the same form called the nonpast form, and the past

tense is expressed by the past form. The context and the use of words such as *today* and *tomorrow* will enable you to distinguish between the present and future tenses. Unlike English, the copula is not used in Japanese passive sentences.

Tanaka-san wa **itsumo** Shushoo ni yobare**masu**.
Mr. Tankaka   always Pr. Min. by   is invited
                                       |
                     nonpast form → present tense

Mr. Tanaka is always invited by the Prime Minister.

Tanaka-san wa **ato de** Shushoo ni yobare**masu**.
             later
                     nonpast form → future tense

Mr. Tanaka will be invited later by the Prime Minister.

Tanaka-san wa **kinoo** Shushoo ni yobare**mashita**.
             yesterday
                     past form → past tense

Mr. Tanaka was invited by the Prime Minister yesterday.

There are two types of passives in Japanese: direct and indirect passives.

Direct (or **regular**) **passive** sentences are similar to passive sentences in English in that the direct or indirect object of the active sentence becomes the subject of the passive sentence. (See **What is a Subject?**, p. 70, and **What are Objects?**, p. 82.)

In direct passives only transitive verbs can be used (see p. 22).

active   Keesatsu wa **hannin o** mimashita.
             policeman   criminal   saw
                | |
             direct object   active verb

The policeman saw the criminal.

passive   Hannin wa keesatsu ni miraremashita.
             criminal   policeman by was seen
              | |
             subject   passive verb

The criminal was seen by the policeman.

active   Sensee wa **gakusee ni** namae o kikimashita.
             teacher   student   name   asked
                      | |
                   indirect object   active verb

The teacher asked the student her name.

passive   **Gakusee wa** sensee ni namae o kikaremashita.
          student   teacher by name   was asked
              │   │
          subject   passive verb
The student was asked her name by the teacher.

Indirect (also called **adversative**) **passives** usually, though not always, indicate that someone is adversely affected by someone else's action or an event. When expressed, the person affected, or the subject, appears at the beginning of the sentence. As in the direct passives, the subject of the active sentence becomes the agent followed by the particle **ni** in the corresponding indirect passives.

In indirect passives intransitive as well as transitive verbs can be used (see p. 22).

- with intransitive verbs

active   Ame **ga** furimashita.
          rain   fell
          │   │
          subject active verb
Rain fell or *It rained.*

passive   **Kodomo wa** ame **ni** furaremashita.
          child   rain by was fallen
          │   │
          subject   agent   passive verb
*My child **was rained on**.*

active   Tomodachi **ga** kimashita.
          friend   came
          │   │
          subject   active verb
My friend came.

passive   **Watashi wa** tomodachi **ni** koraremashita.
          I   friend   by was come
          │   │
          subject   agent   passive verb
*I **was adversely affected** by my friend's coming.*
*My friend came (and **it was inconvenient**).*

- with transitive verbs—Unlike in the direct passives where the direct object in the active sentence becomes the subject of the passive sentence, in the indirect passives a direct object continues to function as a direct object, marked by the particle **o** in both voices.

active   Doroboo ga shujin no **saifu o** nusumimashita.

thief   husband 's wallet   stole

subject   direct object   active verb

*A thief stole my husband's **wallet**.*

passive   Shujin wa doroboo ni **saifu o** nusumaremashita.

husband   thief   by wallet   was stolen

subject   agent   direct object   passive verb

*My husband had his **wallet** stolen by a thief.*

active   Sensee wa **kodomo o** homemashita.

teacher   child   praised

subject   direct object   active verb

*The teacher praised my **child**.*

passive   Sensee ni **kodomo o** homeraremashita.

teacher by   child   was praised

agent   direct object   passive verb

The subject **watashi wa** *(I)* is omitted.

*I had my **child** praised by the teacher.*
*My **child** was praised by the teacher*
(and I was affected by it).

In conversation, as opposed to writing, the subject of a Japanese passive sentence, whether a direct or indirect passive, is usually a person, and not a thing. To translate an English passive sentence with a thing as the subject, as in "My camera was broken by someone," use the indirect passive in Japanese, as in "I had my camera broken by someone," so that the subject will be a person.

Avoiding the Passive Construction

An English passive sentence with a thing (as opposed to a person) as the subject should be expressed by an active sentence in Japanese, especially if it describes a situation that is not unpleasant and no particular person is affected. There are two ways to do this.

1. by using a construction which emphasizes the performer of the action *(as for "x," someone does or did...)*: topic ("x") **wa** + subject **ga** + verb

The exam is written by the teacher.
  | |
subject → thing   agent → performer
→ *As for* the exam, the teacher *writes* it. [performer emphasized]

This bookcase was made by my father.
  | |
subject → thing   agent → performer
→ *As for* this bookcase, my father *made* it. [performer emphasized]

Once you have transformed the English passive sentence into this construction, write it in Japanese.

As for the exam, the teacher writes it.
Shiken wa sensee **ga** kakimasu.
   exam   teacher   writes
    | | |
   topic   subject   active verb

As for this bookcase, my father made it.
Kono honbako wa chichi **ga** tsukurimashita.
  this   bookcase   father   made
    | | |
        topic   subject   active verb

2. by using a construction which does not mention the performer of the action because the performer is regarded as either unimportant or understood *(someone did something and the thing exists in the resultant state)*: **te** form of a transitive verb + the auxiliary verb **arimasu**. You should use this construction when you want to emphasize the state in which something exists as a result of an action.

The door is closed.
  |
subject → thing
→ Someone closed the door and it exists in that state.

The exam was written.
  |
subject → thing
→ Someone had written the exam and it existed in that state.

Once you have replaced the English passive verb form with the **te** form + **arimasu**, write it in Japanese.

To wa (*or* ga) **shimete arimasu.**
   door   close and   exists
    | | |
subject → thing   verb-**te**   auxiliary verb in nonpast
The door is closed.

Shiken wa (or ga) **kaite arimashita**.
    exam   write and   existed
       | | |
subject → thing   verb-**te**   auxiliary verb in past
*The exam **was written**.*

▼▼▼▼▼▼▼▼▼▼▼▼▼▼▼▼▼REVIEW▼▼▼▼▼▼▼▼▼▼▼▼▼▼▼▼▼

I. Underline the subject in the following sentences.
- Circle the performer of the action.
- Identify each sentence as active (A) or passive (P).

1. Everyone will be going away during the vacation.   A   P

2. The bill was paid by Bob's parents.   A   P

3. The bank transfers the money.   A   P

4. The spring break will be enjoyed by all.   A   P

II. Underline the verb in the following sentences in the active voice.
- Identify the tense of the verb: past (P), present (PR), or future (F).
- Write the sentence in the passive voice on the line below.

1. A nurse first questions the patients.   P   PR   F

_____

2. A famous artist painted this picture.   P   PR   F

_____

3. People all over the world will read that article.   P   PR   F

_____

39. WHAT IS THE CAUSATIVE CONSTRUCTION?

The **causative** construction describes a situation in which someone "causes" someone else (or something) to do something. The person who "causes" the situation to come about is usually, at the time, in a position of authority or power over the person who actually performs the action of the verb.

> The mother makes her kids do the homework.

In the above example, *the mother* does not perform the action of the verb, *do the homework*; she just "causes" *her kids* to perform it.

IN ENGLISH
The causative construction consists of the subject + *make*, *have* or *force* + performer + action.

> The coach *made* the team run.
> | | |
>   subject   performer action
> Means: the coach "caused" the team to run.

> The president *has* a secretary write letters.
> | | |
>   subject   performer   action
> Means: the president "causes" a secretary to write letters.

In informal speech *get* is sometimes used instead of *make* or *have* to express a causative meaning.

> I *got* my friend to walk my dog when I was away.
> → I *had* my friend walk my dog when I was away.

A causative meaning can also be expressed by a transitive verb alone, without *make*, *have* or *force*.

> The president *works* the employees hard.
> → The president *makes* the employees work hard.

> I *surprised* my friend.
> → I *caused* my friend to be surprised.

IN JAPANESE
The causative construction consists of the subject **ga** or **wa** + performer **ni** or **o** + action. The performer is marked by the particle **o** when the verb is intransitive and by **ni** when it is transitive (see p. 22). You must know the group to which a verb belongs (**u** verbs, **ru**

verbs, or irregular verbs) in order to choose the proper causative suffix, **aseru** or **saseru** (see **What are Prefixes and Suffixes?**, p. 53, and **What is a Verb?**, p. 21).

A causative verb has a polite and a plain form, a nonpast and a past form, and an affirmative and a negative form (see **What is Meant by Polite and Plain Forms?**, p. 57). Below are examples in the polite affirmative form.

- causative with an intransitive verb

  Koochi **wa** senshu **o** **hashirase***mashita*.
  coach   players   to run - caused
     | | |
  subject   performer   action
  *The coach **made** the players **run**.*

- causative with a transitive verb

  Shachoo **wa** hisho **ni** tegami o **kakase***masu*.
  president   secretary to letter   to write - caused
      | | |
  subject   performer   action
  *The president **has** a secretary **write letters**.*

Careful

Just because the causative construction is used in English does not mean that it will be used in Japanese, and vice versa. For example, the following English sentences, which are not in the causative construction, require the causative construction in Japanese. You must memorize them separately.

*The president **worked** the employees hard.*
→ *The president caused the employees to work hard.*

Shachoo **wa** shain **o** takusan **hatarakase***mashita*.
                             |
                causative form of **hataraku** *(to work)*

*I **surprised** my friend.*
→ *I caused my friend to be surprised.*

Watashi **wa** tomodachi **o** **odorokase***mashita*.
                             |
               causative form of **odoroku** *(to be surprised)*

Causative Verb + Auxiliary Verbs of Doing and Receiving Favors

In Japanese, a causative verb is often used with auxiliary verbs such as **yarimasu** *(do a favor)* and **moraimasu** *(receive a favor)* to soften the harsh tone of the sentence (see **What is an Auxiliary Verb?**, p. 31). In this instance, the causative verb appears in the **te** form. While causative verbs used alone are usually translated into *make, have* and *force* in English, the combination of a causative verb and the auxiliary verbs is translated into *let, allow, permit,* etc.

> Watashi **wa** tomodachi **ni** kuruma **o** unten **sasete yarimashita**.
> I   friend   car   driving   cause to do   did a favor
> *I **let** my friend drive my car.*
> [Literally: *I **did the favor of** having my friend drive my car.*]

> Tanaka-san **wa** kachoo **ni** ichinichi **yasumasete moraimashita**.
> Mr. Tanaka   section chief   one day   cause to rest   received a favor
> *Mr. Tanaka **was allowed** by the section chief to take a day off.*
> [Literally: *Mr. Tanaka **received the favor of** the section chief's allowing him to take a day off.*]

▼▼▼▼▼▼▼▼▼▼▼▼▼▼▼▼REVIEW▼▼▼▼▼▼▼▼▼▼▼▼▼▼▼▼

For each of the following causative sentences circle the performer of the italicized action.

1. The father makes his son *go to work* every day.

2. Yumiko had Tadashi *take pictures* during the trip.

3. I got my roommate *to water* my plants.

40. WHAT IS THE CAUSATIVE-PASSIVE CONSTRUCTION?

As explained in the section **What is the Causative Construction?**, p. 161, the causative construction describes a situation in which someone "causes" someone else to do something. The **causative-passive construction**, on the other hand, describes the same situation, but from the "causee's" point of view: someone is forced to do something by someone else. In other words, it is the passive voice of the causative (active) construction (see **What is Meant by Active and Passive Voice?**, p. 153).

Causative sentence (active) → the subject causes the action

> The clerk made the customer wait.
> subject ("causes") performer action

Causative-passive sentence (passive) → the subject performs the action

> The customer was made to wait by the clerk.
> subject ("performs")   action   agent

In both of the above sentences, the customer waited because the clerk made him do it. The difference between the two sentences is the point of view from which the event is described, *the clerks* point of view in the case of the causative sentence or *the customer's* point of view in the case of the causative-passive sentence.

Causative-passive sentences describe an action that the subject is made to perform against, or regardless of, his or her wishes. In order to understand a causative-passive sentence and a causative sentence, it is important to find out who performs the action expressed by the verb.

IN ENGLISH

The causative-passive construction consists of the subject (i.e., performer) + passive form of ***make*** or ***force*** + action (+ ***by*** + agent). The agent does not have to be expressed.

causative sentence

> The president *forced* the employees to work on Sundays.
> subject ("causes")   performer   action

causative-passive sentence

> The employees *were forced* to work on Sundays by the president.
> subject ("performs")   action   agent

causative sentence

The father *makes* the child clean his room.
subject ("causes")   performer   action

causative-passive sentence

The child *is made* to clean his room by the father.
subject ("performs")   action   agent

Often, the causative-passive construction does not indicate a specific person who "causes" someone to do something. This is true especially when the cause is a particular situation, and not a particular person.

The bus didn't come, so I *was forced* to walk.
situation   action

IN JAPANESE

The **causative-passive** construction consists of the subject (i.e., performer) **ga** or **wa** (+ agent **ni**) + action with the verb in the causative-passive form. You must know the group to which a verb belongs (**u** verbs, **ru** verbs, or irregular verbs) in order to choose the proper causative-passive form, **sareru** or **saserareru** (for the classification of verbs, see **What is a Verb?**, p. 21).

A causative-passive verb has a polite and a plain form, a nonpast and a past form, and an affirmative and a negative form (see **What is Meant by Polite and Plain Forms?**, p. 57). Below are examples in the polite affirmative form.

causative sentence

Tenin **wa** kyaku **o** matase*mashita*.
clerk   customer   to wait - caused
subject   performer   action

*The clerk **made** the customer **wait**.*

causative-passive sentence

Kyaku **wa** tenin **ni** matasare*mashita*.
      (*or* mataserare*mashita*)
customer   clerk   to wait - was caused to
subject   agent   action

*The customer **was made to wait** by the clerk.*

causative sentence

Otoosan **wa** kodomo **ni** heya no sooji o **sase***mashita*.
father   child   room's cleaning do - caused
    | | |_____|
 subject   performer   action
*The father **made** the child **clean** his room.*

causative-passive sentence

Kodomo **wa** otoosan **ni** heya no sooji o **saserare***mashita*.
child   father   room's cleaning do - was caused
  | | |_____|
 subject   agent   action
*The child **was made to clean** his room by his father.*

Careful

Just because the causative-passive construction is used in English, it does not mean that it will be used in Japanese, and vice versa. For example, Japanese usually does not use the causative-passive construction if one is forced to do something due to a situation. Instead, **nakereba narimasen** *(must, have to)* and the like will be used.

Basu ga konakatta kara, **arukanakereba narimasendeshita**.
bus   didn't come so   had to walk
*The bus didn't come, so **I had to (was forced to) walk**.*

On the other hand, some causative-passive sentences are natural in Japanese, but not in English.

Hon o takusan **yomasare**mashita.
             (*or* **yomaserare**mashita).
books   many   was made to read
*I **was made to (I had to) read** many books.*

▼▼▼▼▼▼▼▼▼▼▼▼▼▼▼▼REVIEW▼▼▼▼▼▼▼▼▼▼▼▼▼▼▼▼

For each of the following causative-passive sentences, circle the person who performs the italicized action.

1. Michio was forced *to cook* dinner for his older brother.

2. I am made *to work* twelve hours a day by the manager.

3. We were forced *to invite* everyone to our party.

41. WHAT ARE THE DIFFERENT TYPES OF SENTENCES AND CLAUSES?

Depending on the number and nature of clauses contained, sentences are classified into three major types: simple, compound and complex sentences. Let us look at what distinguishes each type of sentence and how each type is handled in English and Japanese(see **What are Sentences and Clauses?**, p. 89).

Simple Sentence

A **simple sentence** is a sentence consisting of only one clause, or one subject + predicate combination.

IN ENGLISH
Usually the subject comes first, then the main predicate (i.e. verb), and then the rest.

> We stayed home yesterday.
> subject
>   verb

IN JAPANESE
The subject (when expressed) usually comes first, the main predicate (i.e., verb, the copula, or **i**-type adjective) always appears in final position, and the rest in between them.

> (Watashitachi wa) kinoo uchi ni **imashita**.
>   we   yesterday home at stayed
>   subject   verb
> *We **stayed** home yesterday.*

> Shumi wa shashin **desu**.
> hobby   photography is
> subject   copula
> *My hobby **is** photography.*

> Shinkansen wa totemo **hayai desu**.
> Bullet Train   very   is fast
> subject   i-type adj.
>   polite marker
> *The Bullet Train **is** very **fast**.*

Compound Sentence

A **compound sentence** consists of two (or more) equal clauses called **coordinate clauses**. These clauses are joined by words expressing such meanings as *and, but* and *or*.

IN ENGLISH

Two or more coordinate clauses are joined by coordinating conjunctions such as *and, but* and *or* (see **What is a Conjunction?**, p. 49).

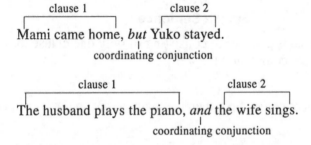

clause 1 clause 2
Mami came home, *but* Yuko stayed.
coordinating conjunction

clause 1 clause 2
The husband plays the piano, *and* the wife sings.
coordinating conjunction

IN JAPANESE

Coordinate clauses are joined by the conjunctive particle **ga** *(but)* or the **te** form of the first main predicate (i.e., verb, copula, and **i**-type adjective). The **te** form literally means *do... and* (with a verb) or *is... and* (with a copula and an **i**-type adjective).

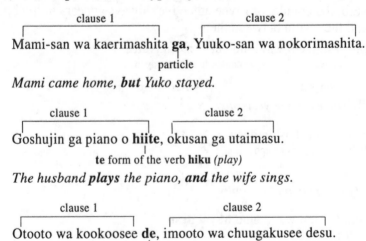

clause 1 clause 2
Mami-san wa kaerimashita **ga**, Yuuko-san wa nokorimashita.
particle
Mami came home, **but** *Yuko stayed.*

clause 1 clause 2
Goshujin ga piano o **hiite**, okusan ga utaimasu.
te form of the verb **hiku** *(play)*
The husband **plays** *the piano,* **and** *the wife sings.*

clause 1 clause 2
Otooto wa kookoosee **de**, imooto wa chuugakusee desu.
te form of the copula **da** *(is)*
My brother **is** *a high school student,* **and** *my sister is a junior high school student.*

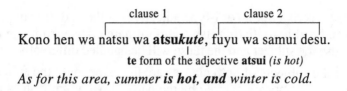

clause 1   clause 2

Kono hen wa natsu wa **atsu*kute*,** fuyu wa samui desu.

te form of the adjective **atsui** *(is hot)*

*As for this area, summer is **hot, and** winter is cold.*

Complex Sentence

A **complex sentence** is a sentence consisting of a main clause and one or more subordinate clauses.

The **main clause** (or **independent clause**) expresses the main idea of a whole sentence. If it stood alone, it could be a simple sentence. The **subordinate clause** (or **dependent clause**) cannot stand alone as a complete sentence; it depends on the main clause for its full meaning.

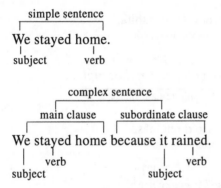

It makes sense to say "We stayed home" without the second clause in the sentence; therefore, it is the main clause. It does not make sense to say, "because it rained" unless we add a conclusion; therefore, it is the subordinate clause.

Subordinate Clauses

IN ENGLISH
Subordinate clauses can be further classified into adverbial, relative, and noun clauses. (Conditional clauses, a type of adverbial clause, are discussed separately, see **What is a Conditional Clause?,** p. 174.) Whatever the type, each clause will have a subject and a verb.

IN JAPANESE
As in English, Japanese has three types of subordinate clauses: adverbial, relative and noun clauses. A subordinate clause will have its main

predicate (i.e., verb, copula, or **i**-type adjective) at the end. It is important that you be able to distinguish a subordinate clause from a main clause because the subject and the tense will be handled differently.

SUBJECT—If the subjects of both clauses are the same, only the subject of the main clause appears marked by the particle **wa** or **ga**. If the subjects are different, the subordinate clause subject must be marked by the particle **ga**, while the main clause subject may be marked by the particle **wa** or **ga**.

TENSE—The way tenses are expressed in subordinate clauses in Japanese is different from English (see **What is Meant by Tense?**, p. 132). For example, no matter what the tense of the whole sentence, the main predicate of the subordinate clause always appears in the nonpast form with **mae ni** *(before)* or in the past form with **ato de** *(after)*.

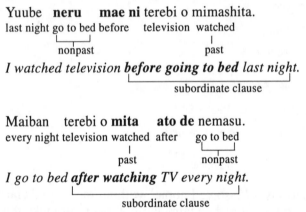

Yuube **neru**   **mae ni** terebi o mimashita.
last night go to bed before   television watched
      └──┬──┘   │
      nonpast   past
*I watched television **before going to bed** last night.*
                        └────────┬────────┘
                        subordinate clause

Maiban   terebi o **mita**   **ato de** nemasu.
every night television watched after   go to bed
            │   └───┬───┘
            past   nonpast
*I go to bed **after watching** TV every night.*
  └──────────┬──────────┘
      subordinate clause

Let us look at what distinguishes each type of subordinate clause and how each type is handled in English and Japanese.

Adverbial Clause

An **adverbial clause** modifies the main predicate of the main clause or the whole main clause. It expresses meanings such as time, reason, concession *(although)*, and condition *(if)* (see **What is an Adverb?**, p. 40, **What is a Conditional Clause?**, p. 174).

IN ENGLISH
An adverbial clause can appear either before or after a main clause. It is headed by conjunctions expressing time *(when, before, after)*, reason *(because, since)*, concession *(although)*, and condition *(if)*.

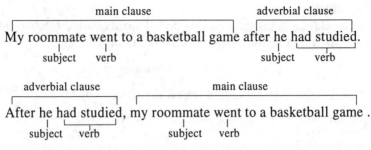

Question: Your roommate went to a basketball when?
Answer: After he had studied.
After he had studied is an adverbial clause expressing time.

IN JAPANESE

An adverbial clause is marked at its end by conjunctive particles such as **kara** *(because)*, **noni** *(although)*, and **ba** *(if)*, or by nouns (+ particles) such as **toki (ni)** *(when)*, **mae (ni)** *(before)* and **ato (de)** *(after)*. The main clause (or at least its main predicate) must appear at the end of the whole sentence.

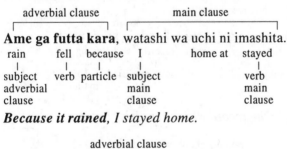

Because it rained, I stayed home.

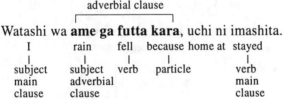

Because it rained, I stayed home.

Relative Clause

A **relative clause** provides additional information about a noun in the main clause which it modifies (see **What is a Relative Clause?**, p. 177).

IN ENGLISH

A **relative clause** is introduced by special words called **relative terms,** such as *which* and *whom,* which follow the noun modified.

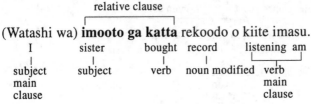

Question: You're listening to which record?
Answer: The one *which my sister bought.*

> *Which my sister bought* is a relative clause modifying the noun *the record.*

IN JAPANESE

A relative clause is not marked by any word; the only clue to detect a relative clause is that its main predicate (i.e., a verb, a copula or an i-type adjective) appears directly in front of a noun.

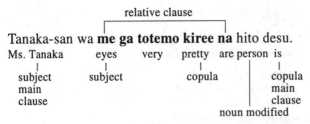

*I'm listening to the record **which my sister bought.***

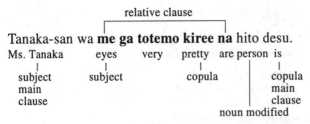

Tanaka-san wa **me ga totemo kiree na** hito desu.

*Ms. Tanaka is a person **whose eyes are very pretty.***

Noun Clause

A **noun clause** functions as a subject or a direct object (see **What is a Subject?**, p. 70, and **What are Objects?**, p. 82).

IN ENGLISH
A **noun clause** is introduced by the conjunction *that*, which can sometimes be omitted.

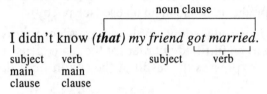

noun clause

I didn't know *(that)* *my friend got married.*

Question: You didn't know what?
Answer: That my friend got married.

> *That my friend got married* is a noun clause functioning as the direct object of the verb *know*.

IN JAPANESE
A noun clause contains the pronouns **koto** or **no** which, unlike the English *that,* cannot be omitted.

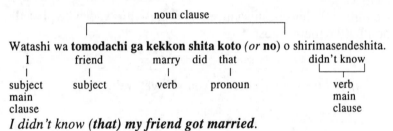

noun clause

Watashi wa **tomodachi ga kekkon shita koto** *(or* **no**) o shirimasendeshita.

I didn't know (that) my friend got married.

▼▼▼▼▼▼▼▼▼▼▼▼▼▼▼REVIEW▼▼▼▼▼▼▼▼▼▼▼▼▼▼▼

Underline the subordinate clauses in the following sentences.

1. While you were out, someone called.

2. We had lots of fun although we got tired.

3. They said that the pictures were ready.

4. Let's go home after we eat.

42. WHAT IS A CONDITIONAL CLAUSE?

A **conditional clause** is a type of subordinate (or dependent) clause, that is, a group of words having a subject and a predicate separate from the subject and predicate of the main clause (see p. 169).

A conditional clause is introduced by words meaning *if* or *unless* and expresses a condition to be fulfilled in order for the main clause to be true. The main clause expresses the result of the condition, called a **conclusion**.

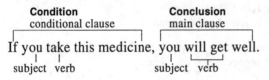

If the condition *you take this medicine* is fulfilled, then the conclusion *you will get well* will be true.

IN ENGLISH

Conditional clauses, introduced by *if* and *unless*, can be placed before or after the main clause.

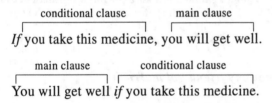

Unless can be substituted for an *if ... not* condition.

If you do *not* come, the man will die.
Unless you come, the man will die.

Careful

When the word "if" is used in the sense of "whether", the clause does not express a condition, but an indirect question (see **What are Direct and Indirect Questions?**, p. 193).

I don't know *if* Ms. Suzuki is coming.
             whether or not

IN JAPANESE

There are four ways to express the meaning "if", by the particles **to**, **nara**, **ba**, and **tara** (see **What is a Preposition?**, p. 44). One of these four conditional markers must be present in a conditional clause. In addition, the adverb **moshi** *(if)* can be placed at the beginning of a conditional clause, but its use is optional.

Unlike the English words *if* and *unless* which appear at the beginning of the conditional clause, the Japanese conditional particles appear at the end of a conditional clause. Moreover, the conditional clause must always be placed before the main clause. The forms, meanings and usages of the four conditional particles are not the same. Refer to your textbook for details. Here is one example of each.

> Kono kusuri o nomu **to**, yoku narimasu.
> this   medicine   take   if   well   get
> |_____| |_____|
>   conditional clause   main clause
>
> *If and whenever you take this medicine, you will get well.*

> Kono kusuri o nomu (**no**) **nara**, yoku narimasu.
> |_____| |_____|
>   conditional clause   main clause
>
> *If you are going to take this medicine as you say, then you will get well.*

> Kono kusuri o nome**ba**, yoku narimasu.
> |_____| |_____|
>   conditional clause   main clause
>
> *If and only if you take this medicine, will you get well.*

> Kono kusuri o non**dara**, yoku narimasu.
> |_____| |_____|
>   conditional clause   main clause
>
> *If (and when) you take this medicine, you will get well.*

There is no equivalent of the word *unless* in Japanese. When you translate, substitute it by *if... not* and use **to**, **ba**, or **tara**.

> *Unless you come, that person will die.*
> → *If you don't come, that person will die.*

> Anata ga konai **to**, ano hito wa shinimasu.
> Anata ga konake**reba**, ano hito wa shinimasu.
> Anata ga konakat**tara**, ano hito wa shinimasu.
> you   not come   if   that person   will die

Counterfactual Condition

When you express a condition that you know is not true, or that is contrary to a fact, it is called a **counterfactual condition**.

IN ENGLISH
Counterfactual statements can be made about the present time or past.

present   If I *had* wings, I *would fly* to you.

Implication: Since I don't have wings, I can't fly to you.

past   If I *had had* wings, I *would have flow*n to you.

Implication: Since I didn't have wings, I couldn't fly to you.

IN JAPANESE
To express a counterfactual condition, in addition to the conditional word at the end of the conditional clause, Japanese uses the particle **noni** *(although, yet)* at the end of a whole sentence. As in English these statements can be made about the present or past time .

present   Tsubasa ga **attara**, tonde **iku noni**.
           wings   exist if fly and go   although
           *If I **had** wings, I **would fly** to you.*

past   Tsubasa ga **attara**, tonde **itta noni**.
           wings   exist if fly and went although
           *If I **had had** wings, I **would have flown** to you.*

▼▼▼▼▼▼▼▼▼▼▼▼▼▼▼▼REVIEW▼▼▼▼▼▼▼▼▼▼▼▼▼▼▼▼▼▼

In each of the following sentences underline a conditional clause, if any.

1. You won't be able to succeed unless you work hard.

2. I'll come running anytime if you need help.

3. I can't decide if I should go to graduate school or not.

4. If I had money, I would travel all over the world.

43. WHAT IS A RELATIVE CLAUSE?

A **relative clause** is a type of subordinate (or dependent) clause, that is, a group of words having a subject and a predicate separate from the subject and predicate of the main clause (see **What are the Different Types of Sentences and Clauses?**, p. 167). A relative clause gives us additional information about a noun, which is called a **head noun** (or simply a **head**). We say the relative clause "modifies" the head.

head   relative clause

The **article** *which I read yesterday* was interesting.

subject verb

As a dependent clause, a relative clause cannot stand alone as a complete sentence. *Which I read yesterday* is not a complete sentence; it modifies the head noun *article* and helps to identify which *article* we are talking about.

IN ENGLISH

A relative clause is usually introduced by a set of words called **relative terms**. They include pronouns *(who, whom, whose, what, which, that)* and adverbs *(where* and *when)*.

When the relative pronoun functions as the subject of the relative clause or as the possessive, it cannot be omitted.

The person ***who*** *plays golf* is Ms. Aoki.

head   relative pronoun, subject of relative clause (must be stated)

You cannot omit *who* and say "*the person plays golf is Ms. Aoki.*"

I met people ***whose*** *children are in Japan.*

head   relative pronoun, possessive (must be stated)

You cannot omit *whose* and say "*I met people children are in Japan.*"

When the relative pronoun functions as a direct or an indirect object, or an object of a preposition, it does not have to be stated. Relative adverbs are also often omitted. In the following examples *whom, which, that,* and *where* are mentioned in parentheses because they can be omitted.

The person (***whom***) *I saw yesterday* was Mr. Suzuki.

head   relative pronoun, direct object (can be omitted)

The article (***which*** or ***that***) *I read yesterday* was interesting.
    head   relative pronoun, direct object (can be omitted)

I went to the same school (***where***) *my sister went.*
               head   relative adverb, place (can be omitted)

As you can see above, the relative clause always comes directly after the noun head that it modifies.

The person *who plays golf* is Ms. Aoki.
    head   relative clause
Who plays golf modifies *the person.*

The word order within a relative clause is the same as in a simple sentence: the subject at the beginning, the verb next, and then the rest.

The person *who plays golf* is Ms. Aoki.
           subject verb direct object

Constructing Relative Clauses

Let us try a few exercises to construct relative clauses. We will turn the first sentence below into a main clause and the second sentence into a relative clause:

sentence A   The letters are interesting.
sentence B   My Japanese friend writes them to me.

1. Identify the element the two sentences have in common: *The letters* and *them*; both words refer to the same thing.
2. Identify the head in sentence A: the letters
3. Word to be replaced by a relative term in sentence B: them
4. Choose the relative term according to the function of the word it replaces and whether it refers to a person or a thing: *them* functions as the direct object of *writes,* and refers to a thing *(letters)*. Therefore, *them* will be replaced with the relative pronoun *which* or *that.*
5. Create the relative clause by starting sentence B with the relative pronoun *(which* or *that)* and place it after the head *(letters).*

The letters ***which*** *my Japanese friend writes to me* are interesting.
The letters ***that*** *my Japanese friend writes to me* are interesting.
    head   relative clause

sentence A	I talked with a woman.
sentence B	She sat next to me on the plane.

1. Common element: *a woman* and *she*
2. Head in sentence A: a woman
3. Word to be replaced by a relative term in sentence B: she
4. Relative term: *she* functions as a subject and refers to a person *who*
5. Relative clause: *who sat next to me on the plane* after *a woman*.

I talked with a woman *who sat next to me on the plane.*
                 head   relative clause

sentence A	I ate dinner at the restaurant.
sentence B	Kim always goes there.

1. Common element: *the restaurant* and *there*
2. Head in sentence A: the restaurant
3. Word to be replaced by a relative term in sentence B: there
4. Relative adverb: *there* functions as an adverb and refers to a place → *where* or *to which*
5. Relative clause: *where* (or *to which*) *Kim always goes* after *the restaurant*.

I ate dinner at the restaurant *where Kim always goes.*
I ate dinner at a restaurant *to which Kim always goes.*
         head   relative clause

In spoken English, you often hear: "I ate dinner at the restaurant Kim always goes to." Notice that the preposition *to* is at the end of the sentence and that there is no relative pronoun or adverb.

IN JAPANESE
Relative clauses in Japanese are very different from those in English. Here are five things to remember.

1. There are no relative terms in Japanese. (Be careful not to use interrogative words such as **dare** *(who?)*, **dare no** *(whose?)* **dore** *(which?)* and **doko** *(where?)*, which are strictly for questions.)

      Gorufu o yaru hito wa Aoki-san desu.
      golf   plays person   Ms. Aoki   is
      relative clause   head

      There is no relative pronoun between the relative clause **gorufu o yaru** *(plays golf)* and the head **hito** *(person)*.

    *The person **who plays golf** is Ms. Aoki.*

Kodomo-san ga Nihon ni iru hito ni aimashita.
children   Japan   in   are   people   met

relative clause   head

*I met people **whose children are in Japan**.*

(Watashi ga) yuube yonda kiji wa omoshirokatta desu.
     I   last night read   article   was interesting

relative clause   head

*The article **which (or that) I read last night** was interesting.*

2. Unlike English where the relative clause comes after the head, in Japanese a relative clause comes directly before the noun head that it modifies.

    Kore wa **kodomo ga yoku miru** bangumi desu.
    this   children   often watch   program   is

         relative clause   head

    Kodomo ga yoku miru *(children often watch)* comes before **bangumi** *(program)*.

    *This is a program **(which) children often watch**.*

3. The word order within a relative clause is the same as in a simple sentence: the subject at the beginning with the particle **ga** (though never **wa**), the main predicate at the end, and the rest in between.

    Kore wa **kodomo ga yoku miru** bangumi desu.
    this   children   often   watch   program   is

         subject   adverb   verb → main predicate

4. The use of particles within a relative clause is the same as in a simple sentence. The only exception is that the particle **wa** cannot be used in a relative clause except for special cases. Therefore, you must use the particle **ga** to mark the subject, if expressed. In the main clause, however, the subject may be marked by either **ga** or **wa**.

    Kore **wa** kodomo **ga** yoku miru bangumi desu.
    this   children   often   watch program   is

subject   subject
(of main   (of relative
clause)   clause)

    You cannot say **kodomo *wa*** within the relative clause.

5. The main predicate within a relative clause must be in the plain form. The only time other forms are used is when the copula is in

the nonpast affirmative. In such a case, what is called the **attributive form** must be used instead of **da**: **no** for the copula attached to a noun and **na** for the copula attached to a **na**-type adjective stem.

relative clause

Kore wa **kodomo ga yoku *miru*** bangumi desu.
this   children   often watch program   is

verb in the plain form
You cannot say **mimasu** (polite form) within the relative clause.
This is a program (which) children often watch.

relative clause

Watashi wa **shiken ga *yasashii*** kurasu o torimasu .
I   exams   are easy   class   will take

i-type adjective in the plain form
You cannot say **yasashii desu** (polite form)
within the relative clause.
I'll take a class in which the exams are easy.

relative clause

Getsuyoobi ga yasumi *no* resutoran wa takusan arimasu .
Mondays   holidays are restaurants   many   there are

copula attached to a noun in the attributive form
You cannot say **yasumi desu** (polite form) or **yasumi da** (plain form) within the relative clause.
There are many restaurants for which Mondays are holidays.

Constructing Relative Clauses

Let us now look at a few examples to see how to construct relative clauses in Japanese. We will use the first sentence as a main clause and the second sentence as a relative clause:

sentence A   Tegami wa omoshiroi desu.
                   The letters are interesting.

sentence B   Nihonjin no tomodachi wa sore o kuremasu.
                   My Japanese friend sends them to me.

1. Identify the element the two sentences have in common: **tegami** *(letters)* in the first sentence and **sore** *(them)* in the second sentence refer to the same thing.

2. Identify the head in sentence A: **tegami** *(letters)*
3. Delete the word in sentence B that refers to the same person or thing as the head, along with the particle that is attached to it. (Remember that there are no relative terms in Japanese.): **sore** *(them)* and **o**
4. Change the particle **wa**, if present in sentence B, to **ga**: **tomodachi** *(friend)* **wa** is changed to **tomodachi ga.**
5. Change the polite form of the verb in sentence B to the plain form: **kuremasu** *(sends to me)* is changed to **kureru.**
6. Place the relative clause before the head: **nihonjin no tomodachi ga kureru** *(my Japanese friend sends to me)* before **tegami** *(letters)*

> **Nihonjin no tomodachi ga kureru** tegami wa omoshiroi desu.
> Japanese   's   friend   sends to me letters   are interesting
> |_____|____|
>   relative clause   head
>
> *The letters (**which**) **my Japanese friend sends to me** are interesting.*

sentence A   (Watashi wa) onna no hito to hanashimashita.
I talked with a woman.

sentence B   Sono hito wa hikooki de tonari ni suwarimashita.
She sat next to me on the plane.

1. Common element: **onna no hito** *(woman)* and **sono hito** *(she)*
2. Head in sentence A: **onna no hito** *(woman)*
3. Delete noun and particle in sentence B: **sono hito** *(she)* and **wa**
4. Change **wa** to **ga**: not applicable (there is no longer **wa** in sentence B see above)
5. Plain form of verb: **suwarimashita** *(sat)* → **suwatta**
6. Placement: **hikooki de tonari ni suwatta** *(sat next to me on the plane)* before **onna no hito** *(woman)*

> (Watashi wa) **hikooki de tonari ni suwatta** onna no hito to hanashimashita.
> I   plane   on next to me sat   woman   with talked
> |_____|____|
>   relative clause   head
>
> *I talked with a woman **who sat next to me on the plane**.*

sentence A   (Watashi wa) resutoran de gohan o tabemashita.
I ate dinner at the restaurant.

sentence A   Kimu-san wa itsumo soko e ikimasu.
Mr. Kim always goes there.

1. Common element: **resutoran** *(restaurant)* and **soko***(tthere)*
2. Head in sentence A: **resutoran** *(restaurant)*
3. Delete noun and particle in sentence B: **soko** *(there)* and **e**
4. Change **wa** to **ga**: Kimu-san **wa** → Kimu-san **ga**
5. Plain form of verb: **ikimasu** *(go)* → **iku**
6. Placement: **Kimu-san ga itsumo iku** *(where Mr. Kim always goes)* before **resutoran** *(restaurant)*

   (Watashi wa) **Kimu-san ga itsumo iku** resutoran de gohan o tabemashita.
     I   Mr. Kim   always goes restaurant at dinner   ate
                       relative clause   head

*I ate dinner at the restaurant **where Mr. Kim always goes**.*

Relative clauses are tricky and this handbook provides only a simple outline. Refer to your Japanese textbook for additional information.

Restrictive and Nonrestrictive Relative Clauses

IN ENGLISH
A **restrictive relative clause** enables us to identify a specific person or thing out of many possibilities. It specifies exactly which head noun is being referred to.

    The movie *(which) I saw last night* was good.
    head   restrictive relative clause

If you simply say, "The movie was good," the listener will not know which movie you are talking about. By adding the relative clause *(which) I saw last night*, you specify (i.e., "restrict") *the movie* and help the listener to identify which one.

A **nonrestrictive relative clause** simply adds information about the head noun. When a relative clause modifies a proper noun, it is usually nonrestrictive. A nonrestrictive relative clause can also be recognized by the presence of commas before and after the clause in writing, and a pause when speaking.

    In Hokkaido, *which is located in the north*, it snows in winter.
    head   nonrestrictive relative clause

The relative clause *which is located in the north* does not help the listener identify which *Hokkaido* you are talking about since there is only one island by that name. Instead of restricting the head, the clause simply adds information. It could be omitted without causing a breakdown in communication.

IN JAPANESE
While the distinction between restrictive and nonrestrictive relative clauses exists in meaning, it is not marked in form. The nonrestrictive clause does not insert a comma or a pause between the head and the clause.

> **Yuube mita** eega wa yokatta desu.
> last night saw   movie   was good
> └─────────────┘   │
>   restrictive   head
>
> *The movie **which I saw last night** was good.*

> **Kita ni aru** Hokkaidoo de wa fuyu ni yuki ga furimasu.
> north in is   Hokkaido   in   winter in snow   falls
> └──────────┘   │
> nonrestrictive   head
>
> *In Hokkaido, **which is in the north**, it snows in winter.*

Headless Relative Clauses

A **headless relative clause** is a relative clause that does not have a specific head noun.

IN ENGLISH
It is easy to identify a headless relative clause because the word preceding the relative clause is not the noun head, as it would be in a regular relative clause. There are two types of headless relative clauses:

1. Relative clauses that start with **what** meaning *that which*.[1]

> relative clause without a head
> ┌──────────────┐
> ***What** he read* was a novel.
> │
> *that which* (does not refer to a specific noun)

> relative clause without a head
> ┌──────────────┐
> ***What** I want to do* is to translate.
> │
> *that which* (does not refer to a specific noun)

---

[1]The relative pronoun **what** (meaning *that which*) should not be confused with other uses of *what*: as an interrogative pronoun *(**What** did you buy?* **Nani** o kaimashita ka, see p. 103), and as an interrogative adjective *(**What** book did you buy?* **Nan no** (or **Donna**) hon o kaimashita ka, see p. 105).

2. Nonrestrictive relative clauses that start with *which* referring to the whole idea expressed in the preceding clause, and not to a specific noun.

relative clause without a head

Mr. Ono doesn't speak English, ***which*** *will be a problem*.

> *Which* refers to the entire previous statement: *Mr. Ono doesn't speak English.*

relative clause without a head

My friend said that kanji is fun, ***which*** *is true*.

> Which refers to the previous statement: *kanji* [Chinese characters] *is fun.*

IN JAPANESE

Japanese does not have either type of headless relative clauses. When a relative clause does not have a specific head, the pronoun **mono**, **koto**, or **no** is added to act as head. The pronoun chosen depends on what is being referred to.

- when referring to objects → **mono** *(thing)* or **no** *(that)*

Otooto ga yonda **mono** (*or* **no**) wa shoosetsu desu.
brother   read   thing   that   novel   is
|_____| |
    relative clause   head

The thing (or ***That***) ***which*** *my brother read was (is) a novel.*
→ ***What*** *my brother read was (is) a novel.*

- when referring to actions, events and facts → **koto** *(thing)* or **no** *(that)*

Watashi ga yaritai **koto** (*or* **no**) wa honyaku desu.
I   want to do thing   that   translation is
|_____| |
    relative clause   head

The thing (or ***That***) ***which*** *I want to do is to translate.*
→ ***What*** *I want to do is to translate.*

It is easy to see that **mono, koto,** and **no** function as heads, because heads always come right after relative clauses in Japanese.

When a relative clause refers to the whole preceding clause, **no desu ga, ga** *(but)*, or the like are used at the end of the preceding clause.

Ono-san wa eego ga hanasenai no **desu ga**, sore wa mondai ni naru deshoo.
Mr. Ono   English   can't speak   **but**   that   problem   become probably
Mr. Ono can't speak English, it will probably become a problem.

Tomodachi wa kanji wa omoshiroi to iimashita **ga**, watashi mo dookan desu.
friend   kanji   fun   that said   **but**   I   too agreement am
My friend said that kanji is fun, I agree.

▼▼▼▼▼▼▼▼▼▼▼▼▼▼▼▼REVIEW▼▼▼▼▼▼▼▼▼▼▼▼▼▼▼▼

I. Underline the relative clause in the following sentences.
▪ Circle the head.

1. The person who speaks Russian is that woman.

2. I am wearing the sweater that my mother knit for me.

3. The man to whom I lent money left the country.

4. Yesterday I read a Japanese novel whose title was "Kitchen".

II. Combine the series of two sentences below into one sentence. (Use the first sentence as a main clause and the second sentence as a relative clause.)
▪ Fill in the blanks showing the steps you have to follow.
▪ On the line below, write the combined sentence.

1. This is a magazine. Young people read it.

(1) Common elements: _____ / _____

(2) _____ is the head.

(3) _____ will be replaced by a relative pronoun.

(4) Relative pronoun: _____

(5) Combined sentence:

_____

2. The new student is nice. He lives across the hall from me.

(1) Common elements: _____ / _____

(2) _____ is the head.

(3) _____ will be replaced by a relative pronoun.

(4) Relative pronoun: _____

(5) Combined sentence:

_____

3. I want to take you to the town. I was born there.

(1) Common elements: _____ / _____

(2) _____ is the head.

(3) _____ will be replaced by a relative adverb.

(4) Relative adverb:_____

(5) Combined sentence:

_____

III. Indicate if following statements about Japanese relative clauses are "True" (T) or "False" (F).

1. The polite form of a verb can be used within a relative clause.

                                                                   T   F

2. A relative clause precedes the noun that it modifies.   T   F

3. The particle **wa** cannot appear in a relative clause except in special cases.   T   F

4. There are no relative pronouns in Japanese.   T   F

44. WHAT ARE DIRECT AND INDIRECT QUOTATIONS?

Direct quotation is the word-for-word transmission of what someone said. It can be a statement, a question, a request, or an order. In writing, the quotation is placed in quotation marks.

statement	Emily said, "I am going to Kyoto."
question	Mr. Aoki asked me, "What did you do yesterday?"
request	I said to my friend, "Please write to me."
order	The doctor said to me, "Sit down."

Indirect quotation is the transmission of what someone said by reproducing the substance of the message. It does not use quotation marks.

statement	Emily said that she was going to Kyoto.
question	Mr. Aoki asked me what I had done the day before.
request	I asked my friend to write to me.
order	The doctor told me to sit down.

A question transmitted in an indirect quotation follows rules of its own and is treated in a separate chapter (see **What are Direct and Indirect Questions?**, p. 193).

IN ENGLISH

When a direct statement, question, request, or order is changed to an indirect quotation several changes are required to reflect the new perspective.

"THAT"—When a statement is changed to an indirect quotation, the conjunction *that* is sometimes used to introduce the indirect quotation. A typical verb used as the main verb is *say*.

Emily *said (that)* she was going to Kyoto.
main verb   conjunction

When a question beginning with an interrogative word is changed to an indirect question, the interrogative word is placed at the beginning of the reported question. A typical verb used as the main verb is *ask*.

Mr. Aoki *asked* me *what* I had done.
main verb   interrogative word

(See **What are Direct and Indirect Questions?**, p. 193, for changes to questions which do not begin with an interrogative word.)

When a request or order is changed to an indirect request or order, *to +* the dictionary form of the verb is usually used for the reported request or order. Typical verbs used as the main verb are *ask, request, tell,* and *order.*

I *asked* my friend *to write* to me.
    main verb   *to* + verb

The doctor *told* me *to sit* down.
    main verb *to* + verb

PRONOUNS—Pronouns such as *I* and *you* in a direct quotation are changed to appropriate pronouns in an indirect quotation to agree logically with the speaker's perspective (for an explanation about personal pronouns see **What is a Personal Pronoun?**, p. 10).

direct quotation   Emily said, "*I* am going to Kyoto."
                      1st person .

indirect quotation Emily said that *she* was going to Kyoto.
                      3rd person

direct quotation   Mr. Aoki asked me, "What did *you* do?"
                              2nd person

indirect quotation Mr. Aoki asked me what *I* had done.
                         1st person

TENSE—The tense of the verb in a direct quotation is independent of the tense of the main clause. The tense of the verb in an indirect quotation, however, depends on the tense of the main clause since it reflects when the reported action took place in relation to the main clause.

Emily *said,* "I *am going* to Kyoto." [*said* and *am going* → same time]
    past   present

Emily *said* that she *was going* to Kyoto. [*said* and *was going* → same time]
    past   past

Mr. Aoki *asked* me, "What *did* you *do*?" [*did do* preceded *asked.*]
    past   past

Mr. Aoki *asked* me what I *had done.* [*had done* preceded *asked.*]
    past   past perfect

TIME AND PLACE—Words referring to a relative time and place, such as *now, tomorrow,* and *here* in a direct quotation, are changed to appropriate words, such as *then, the next day, there* in the indirect quotation to fit the time and place of speaking.

Emily said, "I am going to Kyoto *now.*"
Emily said that she was going to Kyoto *then.*

Mr. Aoki asked me, "What did you do *yesterday*?"
Mr. Aoki asked me what I had done *the day before.*

IN JAPANESE

Other than the fact that a direct quotation is set in quotation marks, the distinction between direct and indirect quotations is not as clear in Japanese as in English.[1]

THE PARTICLE "TO"—Unlike the English word *that* which is only used to introduce the indirect quotation of a statement, the Japanese particle **to** marks both direct and indirect quotations and is placed at the end of the quoted statement, question, request, or order.

- the particle **to** is obligatory with all direct quotations

statement	Emirii-san wa "Kyooto e ikimasu" **to** iimashita.
	Emily Kyoto to go that said
	Emily said, "I am going to Kyoto."

question	Aoki-san wa "Nani o shimashita ka" **to** kikimashita.
	Mr. Aoki what did that asked
	Mr. Aoki asked me, "What did you do?"

request	Tomodachi ni "Tegami o kaite kudasai" **to** tanomimashita.
	friend to letter write please that asked
	I asked my friend, "Please write a letter."

order	Isha wa "Suwarinasai" **to** iimashita.
	doctor sit down that said
	The doctor said, "Sit down."

- the particle **to** is necessary with an indirect quotation whose content is a statement, but optional with a question. The particle **to** is not used with an indirect request or order.

statement	Emirii-san wa Kyooto e iku **to** iimashita.
	Emily Kyoto to go that said
	*Emily said **that** she was going to Kyoto.*

question	Aoki-san wa nani o shita ka (**to**) kikimashita.
	Mr. Aoki what did that asked
	Mr. Aoki asked me what I had done.

[1]In Japanese script, the quotation marks are different from those used in romanization.

PRONOUN—Japanese usually omits pronouns when it is clear from the context who is doing the action. This is also true in direct and indirect quotations. In both sentences below, the subjects in the quotation clauses are not indicated, but understood to be *Emily.*

> **direct quotation**   Emirii-san wa "**Kyooto e ikimasu**" to iimashita.
> *Emily said, "I am going to Kyoto."*

> **indirect quotation**   Emirii-san wa **Kyooto e iku** to iimashita.
> *Emily said that she was going to Kyoto.*

TENSE—Unlike in English, there is no tense agreement between the main clause and the indirect quotation. You simply quote a message in the tense in which it was originally.

> Emirii-san wa Kyooto e **iku** to **iimashita**.
>   nonpast   past
> *Emily said that she is going to Kyoto.*

> Aoki-san wa nani o **shita** ka (to) **kikimashita**.
>   past   past
> *Mr. Aoki asked me what I did (= had done).*

When the content of a quote is a request or order, a nonpast form of a verb + **yoo ni** *(so that)* is usually used. The typical verbs used as the main verb are **tanomimasu** *(ask)* and **iimasu** *(say).*

> **request**   Tomodachi ni tegami o kak u **yoo ni** tanomimashita.
>   friend   to letter   write so that   asked
>   verb + **yoo ni**   main verb
> *I asked my friend to write a letter.*

> **order**   Isha wa (watashi ni) suwaru **yoo ni** iimashita.
>   doctor   me   to   sit down so that   said
>   verb + **yoo ni**   main verb
> *The doctor told me to sit down.*

STYLE—The main predicate (i.e., verb, copula, **i**-type adjective) at the end of an indirect quotation must be in the plain style, regardless of whether it was originally said in the polite or plain style (see **What is Meant by Polite and Plain Forms?**, p. 57).

direct quotation	Emirii-san wa "Kyooto e **ikimasu**" to iimashita.

polite form

Emirii-san wa "Kyooto e **iku**" to iimashita.

plain form

*Emily said "I **am going** to Kyoto."*

Indirect quotation	Emriii-san wa Kyooto e **iku** to iimashita.

plain form

*Emily said she **was going** to Kyoto.*

Time and place—Unlike in English, words such as **ima** *(now)*, **ashita** *(tomorrow)*, and **koko** *(here)* do not have to be changed in the indirect quotation, although they can be.

Emi-san wa Kyooto e **ima** iku to iimashita.
Emi   Kyoto   to now go   that said
*Emily said that she was going to Kyoto **now** (or **then**).*

Aoki-san wa **kinoo** nani o shita ka (to) kikimashita.
Mr. Aoki   yesterday what did   that   asked
*Mr. Aoki asked me what I had done **yesterday** (or **the day before**).*

▼▼▼▼▼▼▼▼▼▼▼▼▼▼▼▼REVIEW▼▼▼▼▼▼▼▼▼▼▼▼▼▼▼▼

Change the direct quotation to indirect quotation in the following sentences.

1. The caller said, "I'm looking for someone from Japan."

_____

2. My mother asked me, "What time did you get back last night?"

_____

3. The policeman said to me, "Move over."

_____

4. I said to the waiter, "Please bring me the menu."

_____

45. WHAT ARE DIRECT AND INDIRECT QUESTIONS?

A **direct question** is a question that is used by itself, independently.

What did Tom do in Japan?
Does Yoko like to dance?

An **indirect** (or **embedded**) **question** is a question inserted in a sentence. It is a type of subordinate (or dependent) clause, that is, a group of words having a subject and a predicate separate from the subject and predicate of the main clause (see **What are the Different Types of Sentences and Clauses?**, p. 167).

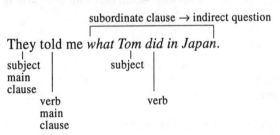

The whole sentence, "They told me what Tom did in Japan," is a statement containing what was orginally the direct question "What did Tom do in Japan?" changed slightly to the indirect question "what Tom did in Japan."

direct question   indirect question

What did Tom do in Japan? → They told me *what Tom did in Japan.*

Here is an additional example.

direct question   indirect question

Does Yoko like to dance? → I don't know *if she likes to dance.*

IN ENGLISH

Indirect questions originate from direct questions. When a direct question begins with an interrogative word *(who, what, where,* etc.), so does an indirect question.

Indirect questions do not have the same form as direct questions: the auxiliary *do* is not required (example 1) and the subject and auxiliary verb are not inverted (example 2). See **What is an Auxiliary Verb?**, p. 31, and **What are Declarative and Interrogative Sentences?**, p. 97.

1. direct question   *What* does Mariko like?
                                           |
                                   auxiliary verb

indirect question   I know *what Mariko likes.*

2. direct question   *Where* will you live?
                                        | | |
                                auxiliary verb + subject + verb

indirect question   Tell me *where you will live.*
                                                | | |
                                subject + auxiliary verb + verb

Within a whole sentence, an indirect question can function as a subject
or a direct object.

> *When he can come* is unclear.
> |
> indirect question → subject of the whole sentence
>   Question: What is unclear?
>   Answer: When he can come.

I don't know *who is coming to the party.*
                                            |
                        indirect question → direct object of *know*
   Question: You don't know what?
   Answer: Who is coming to the party.

When a question with an interrogative word functioning as the subject
is inserted in a sentence, the word order of the question remains the
same.

direct question   *Who* is coming tomorrow?
                              |
                    interrogative word (subject)

indirect question   I don't know *who is coming tomorrow.*

When a *yes*-or-*no* question (i.e., a question without an interrogative
word) is inserted in a sentence, *whether (or not)* or *if...(or not)* is
added at the beginning of the indirect question.

direct question   Did Ms. Kato leave?
                          no interrogative word

indirect question   I don't know *whether (or not)* Ms. Kato left.
                                I don't know *if* Ms. Kato left *(or not).*

IN JAPANESE

Indirect questions in Japanese also originate from direct questions. The word order and the use of particles within an indirect question are the same as in the corresponding direct question.

Interrogative words such as **dare** *(who)*, **nani** *(what)*, and **doko** *(where)* appear where they normally appear, and the particle **ka** is used at the end of the question.

   direct question   Denwa wa **doko ni** arimasu **ka**.
                   phone   where in   is
                               |
                     interrogative word

          Where is the phone?

   indirect question   Denwa wa **doko ni** aru **ka** oshiete kudasai.
                  phone   where in is   tell   please
                             |
                     interrogative word

          *Please tell me **where** the phone is.*

The main predicate (i.e., verb, copula, **i**-type adjective) at the end of an indirect question must be in the plain style, regardless of whether it was originally asked in the polite or plain style (see **What is Meant by Polite and Plain Forms?**, p. 57).

   direct question   Denwa wa doko ni **arimasu** ka.
                                   |
                         polite style verb

          Where is the phone?

   indirect question   Denwa wa doko ni **aru** ka oshiete kudasai.
                               |
                       plain style verb

          *Please tell me where the phone **is**.*

As in English, an indirect question can function as a subject or a direct object. While the particle **ga** is usually retained marking an indirect question as the subject of the main clause, the particle **o** marking it as the direct object is usually omitted. We have, therefore, indicated **o** between parentheses in the examples below.

   Itsu korareru ka ga mondai desu.
   when can come   question is

   indirect question → subject of the whole sentence
   ***When he can come** is the question.*

Dare ga paatii e kuru ka (o) shirimasen.
who   party to come   don't know

indirect question → direct object of **shirimasen** *(don't know)*

*I don't know **who is coming to the party**.*

When a *yes*-or-*no* question (i.e., a question without an interrogative word) is inserted in a sentence, **doo ka** *(whether or not)* is added at the end of the indirect question.

direct question	Katoo-san wa kaerimashita ka. no interrogative word *Did Ms. Kato leave?*
indirect question	Katoo-san wa kaetta **ka doo ka** shirimasen. Ms. Kato left whether or not don't know *I don't know **whether or not** Ms. Kato left.*

▼▼▼▼▼▼▼▼▼▼▼▼▼▼▼▼REVIEW▼▼▼▼▼▼▼▼▼▼▼▼▼▼▼▼▼

I. Underline the indirect question in each of the following sentences.

1. Shall we ask what they're serving tonight?

2. I can't decide whether I want to see the movie or not.

3. Tell me whom you like the most.

4. I wonder if there are any tickets left.

II. Combine the series of two sentences below into one sentence and write the combined sentence on the line.

1. I don't know. When was this temple built?

_____

2. Please tell me. Will the store be open tomorrow?

_____

ANSWER KEY

1. **What is a Noun?** 1. spring day, Joe, Nancy, Smith, Kyoto, train 2. Smiths, temple, mountain 3. temperature, view 4. cherry trees, birds 5. garden, children, school uniform 6., hearts, joy, happiness 7. couple, pictures 8. postcards, friends, America

2. **What is a Pronoun?** 1. you, me 2. I, him 3. they, it 4. her, us

4. **What is Meant by Number?** 1. hon, pon, bon 2. ri, nin 3. mai 4. tsu 5. hiki, piki, biki 6. tsu 7. ri, nin 8. hiki, piki, biki 9. hon, pon, bon

5. **What is the Possessive?** 1. Akira 2. sweater 3. school 4. car 5. magazines

6. **What is a Verb?** 1. runs 2. were 3. enjoyed, preferred 4. ate, finished, went 5. realized, has 6. felt, seems 7. stayed, expected 8. was, see, struggle, get 9. increases, remains

7. **What are the Uses of the Verb "To be"?** I. 1. is, 'm 2. were 3. was 4. 're, is 5. is, 's II. 1. Yes 2. No 3. No 4. Yes 5. No

8. **What is an Auxiliary Verb?** 1. Did 2. will 3. Do 4. Have

9. **What is an Adjective?** 1. noun 2. descriptive 3. interrogative 4. demonstrative

10. **What is a Descriptive Adjective?** 1. exciting → game 2. young → woman; crowded → train 3. tired → We, long walk 4. great → Bill dark → suit 5. warmer → earth

11. **What is an Adverb?** 1. quite → early, early → arrived 2. really → quickly, quickly → fixed 3. too → long 4. reasonably → secure 5. very → well, well → speaks

12. **What is a Preposition?** 1. about, among 2. from 3. beside 4. at, by 5. to 6. for

13. **What is a Conjunction?** 1. and, Yoshiko, Mami, or, Boston, New York 2. but, I did my homework, my dog ate it 3. so, Mr. Tanaka has to borrow money, he can buy a car 4. when, My friend is supposed to call me, she gets home

15. **What are Prefixes and Suffixes?** I. 1. **un**certain 2. **en**large 3. **mis**understand 4. **re**pay 5. **de**code II. 1. grace**ful** 2. sleep**less** 3. work**er** 4. short**en** 5. depend**s**

21. **What is a Subject?** 1. Q: Who started playing music? A: the band Q: Who came out? A: all the players 2. Q: Who took the order? A: one waiter Q: Who brought the food? A: another waiter 3. Q: Who voted for the class president? A: the students 4. Q: Who is always right? A: my mother 5. Q: What may be difficult? A: it Q: What is an interesting language? A: Japanese

22. **What is a Topic?** 1. topic → yesterday; subject → who, Chris 2. topic → algebra; subject → I 3. topic → last year; subject → the Suzukis 4. topic → Japan; subject → Japan

23. **What is a Predicate?** 1. predicate → is my favorite season; main predicate → is 2. predicate → are quite expensive; main predicate → are 3. predicate → sponsored a wonderful exhibit with the central theme of world peace; main predicate → sponsored

24. **What are Objects?** I. 1. Q: The children brought what? A: a kitten → DO 2. Q: The Red Cross sends what? A: food and medical equipment → DO, Q: The Red Cross sends food and medical equipment to whom? A: to people in need → IO 3. Q: The parents paid for what? A: the books → OP; Q: The parents paid with what? A: a credit card→ OP

26. **What are Affirmative and Negative Sentences?** 1. Masashi does not (or doesn't) speak French. 2. I do not (or don't) exercise every day. 3. Japanese grammar is not (or isn't) difficult. 4. The winds were not (or weren't) strong last night. 5. We will not (or won't) go sailing tomorrow.

27. **What are Declarative and Interrogative Sentences?** I. 1. Did Hajime and Yoshiko study all evening? 2. Does Mr. Honda work for an automobile company? 3. Will California be dry this summer? II. 1. What is Akira studying in college? 2. When did they live in Arizona? 3. Who likes to sing karaoke? III. 1. They are planning to raise taxes, aren't they? 2. It doesn't snow around here, does it? 3. The new movie is very funny, isn't it?

28. **What is an Interrogative Word?** I. 1. What → DO 2. What → S 3. Whose → POSS II. 1. dore 2. dochira 3. dono hito III. 1. What → time 2. Which → hotel IV. 1. When 2. Why 3. How

29. **What is a Demonstrative Word?** I. 1. kore 2. sore 3. are 4. places II. 1. that → candidate 2. this → food 3. those → sneakers 4. these → houses III. 1. that → well 2. this → hard 3. this way → fold

30. **What are Indefinite and Negative Pronouns?** 1. somebody
2. Nobody 3. anything, Nothing 4. anything 5. Anyone

31. **What are Indefinite and Negative Adverbs?** 1. somewhere
2. anywhere 3. never 4. sometime 5. anytime 6. nowhere

32. **What is Meant by Tense?** I. (1) time (2) simple (3) two
(4) auxiliary (5) main (6) present (7) past (8) past (9) future
II. 1. PR, NP 2. P, P 3. F, NP

33. **What is the Present Tense?** I. (1) masu (2) masen (3) desu
(4) dewa arimasen (5) ja arimasen (6) i desu (7) ku arimasen
(8) ku nai desu II. 1. Same 2. Different 3. Different

34. **What is the Future Tense?** I. (1) present (2) masu (3) masen
(4) ni (5) ni (6) ku (7) ku

35. **What is the Past Tense?** I. (1) mashita (2) masendeshita
(3) deshita (4) dewa arimasendeshita (5) ja arimasendeshita
(6) katta desu (7) ku arimasendeshita (8) ku nakatta desu
II. 1. Different 2. Same 3. Different

36. **What is the Progressive?** 1. Yes 2. Yes 3. No 4. Yes 5. No

37. **What is the Imperative?** I. 1. Practice the piano every day.
2. Let's take a bus tour. II. 1. IMP 2. IMP 3. NP 4. NP 5. IMP

38. **What is Meant by Active and Passive Voice?** I. 1. subject →
everyone; performer → everyone; A 2. subject → the bill; performer → Bob's parents; P 3. subject → the bank; performer → the
bank; A 4. subject → the spring break; performer → all; P
II. 1. verb → questions; tense → present; passive → The patients are
first questioned by a nurse. 2. verb → painted; tense → past; passive → This picture was painted by a famous artist. 3. verb → will
read; tense → future; passive → That article will be read by people
all over the world.

39. **What is a Causative Construction?** 1. his son 2. Tadashi
3. my roommate

40. **What is a Causative-Passive Construction?** 1. Michio 2. I
3. we

41. **What are the Different Types of Sentences and Clauses?**
1. While you were out 2. although we got tired 3. that the pictures
were ready 4. after we eat

42. **What is a Conditional Clause?** 1. unless you work hard 2. if you need help 3. none 4. If I had money

43. **What is a Relative Clause?** I. 1. who speaks Russian; head → The person 2. that my mother knit for me; head → the sweater 3. to whom I lent money; head → the man 4. whose title was "Kitchen"; head → a Japanese novel II. 1. (1): a magazine/it, (2) a magazine, (3) it, (4) which (or that), (5) This is a magazine which (or that) young people read. 2. (1): the new student/He, (2) the new student, (3) He, (4) who, (5) The new student who lives across the hall from me is nice. 3. (1) the town/there (2) the town (3) there (4) where (5) I want to take you to the town where I was born. III. 1. F 2. T 3. T 4. T

44. **What are Direct and Indirect Quotations?** 1. The caller said that he (*or* she) was looking for someone from Japan. 2. My mother asked me what time I had gotten back the night before. 3. The policeman told me to move over. 4. I asked the waiter to bring me the menu.

45. **What are Direct and Indirect Questions?** I. 1. what they're serving tonight 2. whether I want to see the movie or not 3. whom you like the most 4. if there are any tickets left II. 1. I don't know when this temple was built. 2. Please tell me whether or not (*or* if) the store will be open tomorrow.

INDEX

NOTES